BRITISH ISLES
IRELAND

A HEDONIST PRODUCTION

Western Scotland / Pete Adams

HOW TO USE WAVE-FINDER

How does Wave-Finder Work?
Wave-Finder uses mini **data-maps** and **icons** to help you quickly identify the best conditions for each break. The icons also indicate wave type and direction; see opposite.

What do I look at first?
You can find your desired break by looking at the area map for each section. Find out what area you are in by looking at the contents pages overleaf. There's also a break index at the back.

How do I find the best spot for the conditions?
Each spot has its own **data-map** showing the main streets and landmarks nearest the break. Look for the **icon box** located in the corners. This contains info on Wave direction, bottom type, best swell direction, best tide, and best wind direction.

Wave locators in each map show position and direction of wave. There may be more than 1 break per map; in this case you'll see 2 or more icon boxes, each relating to the nearest locator. If you know the current wind direction (or other conditions), you can flick through the maps and scan the icons.

Scale marked on map relates to the 2cm scale bar. In this case the bar is 1.5 kilometres so the whole map is about 3k long. All maps face **north** but scales **vary** in order to fit important features in.

Tides: Most maps show beach at low tide, with a black line for the high tide mark. This is why some waves appear on the rocks, because that's where they break on a higher tide.

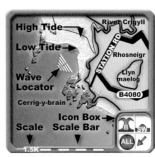

Additional Info
Surf **data-charts** for each ocean zone show seasonal conditions & hazards etc. There's a forecasting page at the back, or check:
www.wave-finder.com.

ICON EXPLANATION

Wave Locator
Shows wave pos -ition & direction

| Left | Right | A-Frame | R Point | L Point |

Wave Type - Wave icon shows direction, letter in center shows bottom type. See Below.

Icon	Description	Icon	Description
R	Right, R = Reef bottom	B	Right Left Beach break
S	Right, S = Sandbar/River	P	Left, P = Pointbreak

Swell Direction - Shows **best** swell direction. **Other swell directions may also work for this wave.**

N	North swell is best	SE-SW	SE-SW is best
NW-W	NW -W is best	SW	SW is best

Best Tide - Shows **Optimal** tide heights. **Can change subject to sand movement and swell direction. Other tides may work.**

Icon	Description	Icon	Description
(	Low is best	●	High is best
(	Mid is best	)	Low - Mid is best

Best Wind - Shows wind direction for a **perfect** off-shore. Long curved beaches will show a range of directions.

Icon	Description	Icon	Description
→	Westerly (from West)	↘	North to Westerly
↗	Southwesterly	←	Easterly

Special Icons - You will find these against certain spots on area maps. They indicate **exceptional** features about the break.

Icon	Description	Icon	Description
!	Handles huge swells	P	Protected from winds
∩	Swell Magnet	★	World Class Wave

" Balin // - Provider of all that is good in Surfers Hardware "

balun
AUSTRALIAN MADE FOR 30 YEARS

European head office, Oakland.
tel +44 (0)1566784444. fax +44 (0)1566784555.
Email sales@oaklandimports.com

As far from town as can be / Pete Adams

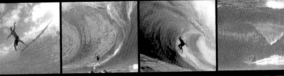

SAVE OUR SPORT

How can an amazing, natural phenomena of a sport such as ours be in danger? 2 principal threats, both with a solution:

Crowds

There are more of us every day and the water's getting busy. As an editorial team, we have to weigh up the pros and cons of telling you about places to go surf. By informing you about the best conditions for a given spot, no additional surfers are created: the same crew just get sent to a better spot. Nevertheless, the balance is changed. You'll be a plus 1 there and a minus 1 somewhere else. If you can be low-impact then both spots benefit...simple!

For this reason we ask you to be a little bit respectful when you visit somebody's backyard. Obey some basic rules: - **don't paddle out in a crowd of you** - **don't snake or drop in** - **skirt the main peak** for a while before steaming in - **park your car carefully** - **shut gates**.

We also hope that locals in that spot can appreciate that they too might need to go on a journey some day. When our chief scribe Larry Blair first won the Pipeline Masters, local hard-man Brian Surat speared his board because he was not Hawaiian. I don't think Brian's tactic has reduced the crowd at Backdoor or Rockpile.

Sometimes however, quiet little spots that cannot handle numbers (like reefs or points) flicker on our editorial radar. We keep many of these out so that you can have the joy of "discovering" them. A large number of good breaks fell into this category and we have kept them secret.

Pollution

For years, the aquatic environment has been viewed as a bottomless pit for human derived waste. Millions of gallons of raw or partially treated sewage are discharged around the UK coastline each day. Though less raw sewage is now dumped in the ocean our water environment remains under pressure from a cocktail of toxic chemicals that bypass the sewage treatment works and settle in the marine environment ultimately threatening the health of wildlife and humans alike. Since 1990, **Surfers Against Sewage** have led the charge to create awareness and win legislation to prevent our playground (and the home of all our fish) from being totally destroyed. If you care about the future of your sport and food supply, check their site and join up: **www.sas.org.uk** or tel: **0845 4583001**.

Shapes and designs by :::

Made by ::: RESIN8™ Ridd

TRIED AND TESTED INSIDE JAH GLIDE WORLD WIDE
BY EUGENE TOLLEMACHE ::: ENGLISH NATIONAL CHAMPION

M EGAN
by :: YOU
RESIN8
SURFBOARD INNOVATORS
in8.com.au
OCEAN THERAPY AT resin8.com.au

FOREWORD

We set out to provide the most compact, comprehensive, easy to use guide for the travelling surfer. Our aim is that wherever you find yourself in the UK and Ireland, and whatever the conditions, you will easily be able to find a quality spot nearby.

Taking the adventure and discovery out of surfing is not one of our aims. Our coast-line is so convoluted and complex that secret spots are tucked away in corners everywhere. We have no intention of diluting the pleasure of stumbling upon these havens by exposing them. Many spots get removed from wave-finder for this reason, and because we endeavour to respect the secrecy of certain surf havens.

We are however, pointing you towards some of the best surfing locations in this diverse, rugged land of the UK and Ireland. In return, we ask you to respect the surfers who live in each area, and be merciful to the natural environment.

The icon and data-map system is designed to save time and get you quickly and simply to the right spot for the conditions. Bear in mind that any break can be great on its day, and banks can re-align between swells to give perfect, but short-lived perfection; Therefore expect the unexpected.

We send heartfelt thanks to the many dozens of surfers who have contributed their sketches, words, photos and time.

Shore-break / Bernie Baker

WELCOME TO THE ROCK!

SALT ROCK .COM

"team rock"

H.Q. VELATOR BRAUNTON UK T> +44 (0) 1271 815306

CONTENTS

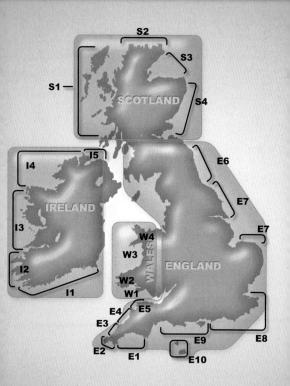

CONTENTS

CONTENTS

Editorial, Contributors, Art and Photos

Larry Blair, Adam Coxen, Jeremy Goring, Jo Oliver, Peter Adams, Jim Michell, Jim Brooks-Dowsett, Lewis Arnold, Justin Sharp, Ben Granata, Alex Liddle, Chris Adams, Nick & Sarah Baron, Hilton Dawe, Tim McKenna, Andy Hill, Richie Fitzgerald, Jamie Russell, Dominic Boletta, Bernie Baker, Remy Whiting, Luke Young, Wes Baker, Steve Darch, Suzie Keane, Anne O'Brien, Richard Hardy, Ian Black

Pipeline Master Larry Blair on assignment, Hebrides / Pete Adams

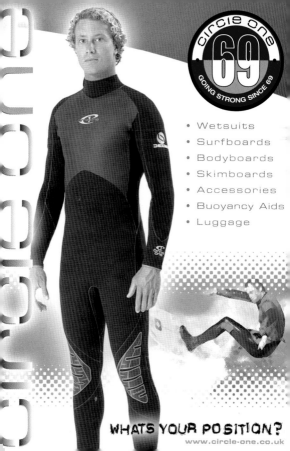

UK IRELAND: SWELL MAP

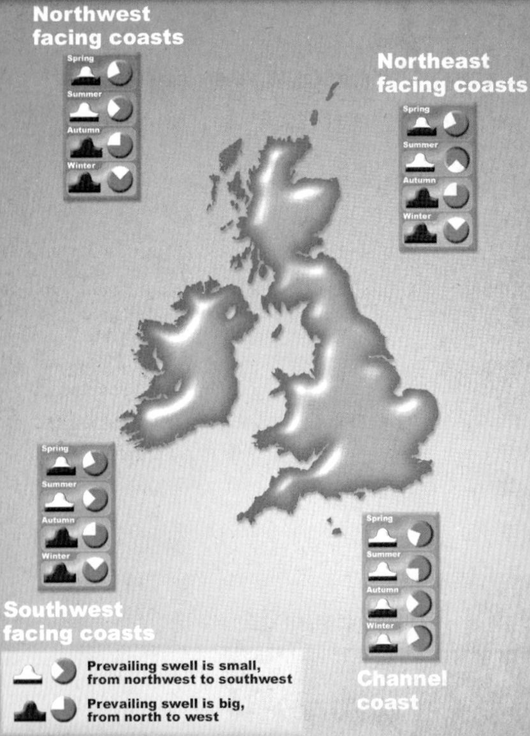

Northwest facing coasts

Spring
Summer
Autumn
Winter

Northeast facing coasts

Spring
Summer
Autumn
Winter

Southwest facing coasts

Spring
Summer
Autumn
Winter

Channel coast

Spring
Summer
Autumn
Winter

Prevailing swell is small, from northwest to southwest

Prevailing swell is big, from north to west

Look at swell window to get seasonal overview of prevailing swell direction and size for each coast.

MICK FANNING
GRIFTER
DRAGONOPTICAL.COM

ENGLAND

Somewhere West / Jim Michell / barefootmedia.co.uk

ENGLAND

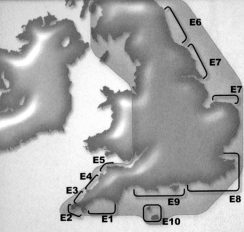

SOUTHWEST SURF DATA

Background

The birthplace of UK surfing. Cornwall is blessed with beautiful land-scape and coastline, plus an array of surfable beaches, reefs and a few not so secret point-breaks. It gets more and more crowded every year but the patient explorer will be rewarded. Neighboring Devon has always competed for the honours; whilst sometimes less consistent, it hosts some quality setups.

When to go

Summer: Often flat, on-shore and crowded, it's a frustrating time to be in Cornwall. Generally only the more exposed beaches will get swell at this time, and these are prone to on-shore breeze from the southwest. **Autumn**: Power swells emanate from north Atlantic lows. When these storms track far enough south for long enough, the resulting swell powers into Cornwall's north coast. The larger more south-going fronts also liven up the south coast. Late autumn is best! **Winter**: More swell, colder water, uncrowded waves; a perfect time for the hard core. Quality corner spots ignite with these bigger swells. **Spring**: Swell pattern becomes more spread out, and the water is at its coldest, but some great spring sessions are to be had. With the exception of Easter, uncrowded days are common. Check the forecast before you go or its clotted cream and warm beer for you.

Hazards

Crowds, cold winter water, flat spells. Traffic and crowds of kooks increase yearly.

M	Swell Range		Wind Pattern		Air		Sea	Crowd
	Feet	Dir'	Am	Pm	Lo	Hi		
J	2-8	nw	variable	sw	-2	10	8-9	low
F	2-8	nw	variable	sw	-2	10	8-9	low
M	2-6	nw	variable	sw	3	13	10	low
A	2-6	nw-w	variable	sw	6	16	11	med
M	2-5	nw	variable	sw	9	17	13	med
J	1-3	nw-sw	variable	sw	13	23	14	hi
J	1-3	nw-sw	variable	sw	15	25	16	hi
A	1-3	nw-sw	variable	sw	15	25	16	hi
S	1-9	nw-w	variable	sw	13	24	16	med
O	2-9	nw	variable	sw	12	18	15	med
N	2-9	nw	variable	sw	8	14	14	low
D	2-9	nw	variable	sw	4	12	10	low

NOT ONLY ARE YOU CATCHING WAVES.

Viruses such as Hepatitis A can survive for up to 100 days in sea water.

Join the SAS campaign today 0845 4583001. www.sas.org.uk

surfers against sewage

E1: CORNWALL & DEVON SOUTH

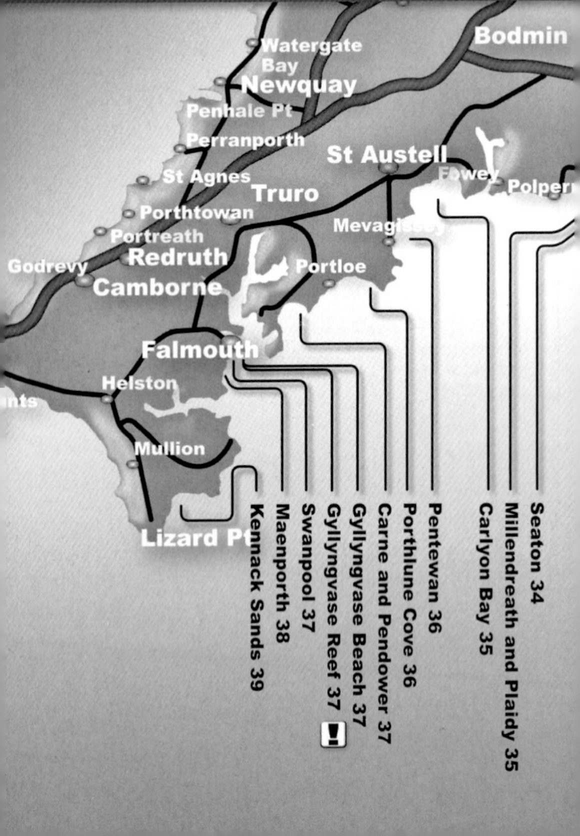

Bodmin

Watergate Bay
Newquay
Penhale Pt
Perranporth
St Agnes
St Austell
Fowey
Polper
Truro
Porthtowan
Mevagissey
Portreath
Redruth
Godrevy
Portloe
Camborne

Falmouth
Helston
nts

Mullion

Lizard Pt

Kennack Sands 39
Maenporth 38
Swanpool 37
Gyllyngvase Reef 37
Gyllyngvase Beach 37
Carne and Pendower 37
Porthlune Cove 36
Pentewan 36
Carlyon Bay 35
Millendreath and Plaidy 35
Seaton 34

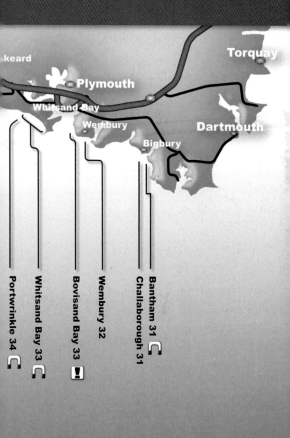

keard

Torquay

Plymouth

Whitsand Bay

Wembury

Dartmouth

Bigbury

Portwrinkle 34

Whitsand Bay 33

Bovisand Bay 33

Wembury 32

Bantham 31

Challaborough 31

BANTHAM

West from Churchstow on the A379, fork left after 2km. Follow road all the way into Bantham. Or approach from the Challaborough side on B3392.

Lined up rivermouth break that is quite consistent relative to south coast breaks, and offers a little bit of power if there is a major swell. The middle of the bay has a left-right peak, with rights often reeling for a distance. Some more rights can be found towards the island. Solid west swells and north to east winds are best. 1-8ft. Rips can be bad. All levels unless big. Beautiful. One of the best spots on the South Devon coast.

CHALLABOROUGH

Head north out of Bigbury. Follow Challaborough signs. Parking at the beach.

Right-hand rock/sand point at the north end that can provide hollow power waves on solid west swells and NW - NE winds. There's a jump-off spot if you want to avoid the paddle, but watch locals before you make the decision. Beach-break Lefts & Rights too, on lower tides in the middle, in north to east winds. 1-6ft plus. Generally an advanced spot if its really happening.

31

WEMBURY

Head east from Plymouth on the A379. Right turn at Elburton, then Wembury Rd south. Follow Wembury signs. Parking at end of Cliff Rd.

Known for **The Point**: Long flat-rock left that wraps off the rocks on higher tides. It may not get big too often, but it can have good shape, reasonable power and long walls. Needs XL southwest swell for it to work properly. Can get good on those rare days.

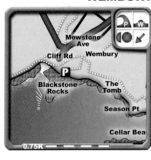

Most tides are OK here, but higher is better. If on, it will be crowded unless you're the first to catch it. LR beach-break peaks in the bay at low tide which can close out. Crowds. Advanced if big. 1-8ft.

BOVISAND BAY

From Plymstock to Hooe, then take Staddon Lane for about 3k south.

Rare reef breaks work through the tides although mid is best; too low and it can dry-suck. Likes SW swell & NE-E wind. If it is working there will be a tight local crew, and this combined with a restricted take-off zone makes for difficult sessions at times. Advanced. 2-8ft.

From Plymouth get over to Torpoint and follow A374 to Antony. Head S on the B3247. Take Freathy turn-off left, and then right for Military Rd which runs behind the beach. Numerous access points to the sand so check for the best peaks.

Whilst this spot is one of the most popular south coast surf zones, it is so expansive that you will often find a peak to yourself, if it's on. It's one of the more consistent beach-breaks in the area but still needs a solid southwest to west swell to break. The rule of thumb is that the further east you go, the more swell you might get. Peaks all across the strip, notably **Tregantle Cliff**, **Tregonhawke** and **Sharrow** on lower tides. Tregantle is military so be aware. Holds from 1 to 8ft and can generate power on the rare 4ft plus days. There's a mysto reef out from **Queener Point** that can get good and hollow. Prevailing south-westerly winds are on-shore. All levels. Currents when big, so becomes intermediates plus. Crowds variable although quiet during the week.

PORTWRINKLE

Access off the B3247, at the west end of Whitsand Bay.

Western end of an enormous stretch of beachbreak. The Portwrinkle end hosts some patchy sand covered rock setups that work on all tides in very big SW or huge W swells. High tide is a bit rocky. The Tregantle Cliff end of the strip is more consistent, pretty good quality beach-break, and also works through the tides.

SEATON

Head west towards Looe from Portwrinkle on B3247. Its after Downderry.

If the paddle-out at Whitsand is looking a bit heavy then Seaton is worth a look. The pebble and rock strewn beach has a rivermouth at its west end and it can have good low tide banks on a very big west swell or huge winter swell. 1-4ft. Inconsistent. All levels.

MILLENDREATH AND PLAIDY

From East Looe, head E on Plaidy Park Rd to the end.

Out of the way, scenic little pair of beaches but you need a lot of luck if you are to get them working. Usually pretty small here, with low tide the best chance. Needs a very big west to southwest ground-swell to produce the goods. Inconsistent. Uncrowded. 1-5ft. All levels.

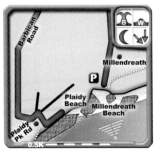

CARLYON BAY

Head E from St Austell on the A390, and branch off right on B3082(Par Moor Rd). Signs to Cornwall Coliseum.

Incredibly mellow learners spot. Get your foamy and go! Low to mid tide chop will be good for beginners, unless huge west swell penetrates this far up the Channel, when waves of reasonable power can appear. Likes any north wind. 1-4ft. Only crowded in summer, and then it's mostly polystyrene and grans. Beginners and golfers.

35

North of Mevagissey on the B3273. R into Pentewan just before Barton Farm.

A more inconsistent spot barely exists, but on a very rare big SW swell or an absolute monster W, this spot will yield some small waves protected from west winds. When it is on you need a middle tide or higher, as low tends to kill what little power there is. Check the point in the S, and the rivermouth up N. Will also deliver wind-chop from the English Channel on those rare strong easterlies, if they have blown hard enough for long enough. 1-5ft. Pretty place, great for beginners.

PORTHLUNE COVE

Wind your way west from Mevagissey through Tregavarras and St Michael Caerhays. A mission to get to.

Scenic, fickle beach-break that picks up either a very solid southwest groundswell, or any east Channel wind-swell. There are lefts and rights on all tides, and an off-shore sand-bank at the western end. On rare bigger days from 3-5ft, it gets pretty hollow. 1-5ft. Rarely crowded. All levels. Incredible natural beauty and crusty old castle. Beach disappears at high tide.

CARNE AND PENDOWER BEACHES

Head about 10k north from St Mawes on the A3078. Take Rocky Lane right for Carne just before Treworlas, park near hotel.

One of the last severely protected beaches on the way west, this is another spot that requires very big, rare southwest ground-swell to generate anything rideable. When on, expect peaky little beach-break pulses in a beautiful setting. Any tide OK, just make sure all else is massive before you bother checking it. 1-4ft. All levels. Uncrowded. Fickle.

GYLLYNGVASE & SWANPOOL BEACHES

At the southeast end of Falmouth. Gyllyngvase is at the west end of Cliff Rd (bottom of Gyllyngvase Hill), Swanpool is at the bottom of Swanpool Rd.

Gyllyngvase beach rarely has a wave and if on will be terribly crowded; its the town beach with all the facilities that go with it. 1-4ft. Beginners. **The Reef** or **Point** (west end of beach) is a good, rare right at mid to high tide, requiring major southwest swell and a northwest wind. If on, it'll be steep and punchy. **Swanpool** is a rocky, protected cove that picks up channel chop or huge south-oriented swells.

MAENPORTH

From Falmouth Town Ctr, head south on A39, find Swanpool Rd then bottom of Maenporth Rd.

Rare, pretty little cove slightly out of town. Needs those E channel wind swells to have a wave, unless a very solid SW is getting in. The main advantage: it's off-shore in westerly winds. If it's on there'll be a crowd onto it quite fast, but winter is best if you want to avoid the varied surf craft and swimmers. The waves are generally improvers level although rocks complicate things slightly. Rare, but a life-saver when huge swells obliterate open beaches.

KENNACK SANDS

Head south from Helston on the A3083 past Mullion, take left through Ruan Major and Kuggar. Footpath to the beach.

Another spot to check on massive but rare south-west swells and any west or north winds. Kennack's beautiful sand beach produces occasional quality beach break action, mostly on lower tides. High is extra fat and cuts the beach in 2. Good for beginners, and rarely crowded unless firing on a weekend. 1-5ft. Fickle! Close-outs common.

39

E2: CORNWALL WEST

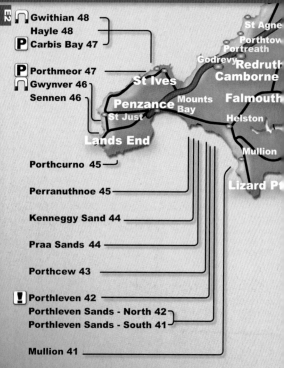

E2

🅿 Gwithian 48
Hayle 48
🅿 Carbis Bay 47

🅿 Porthmeor 47
Gwynver 46
Sennen 46

Porthcurno 45

Perranuthnoe 45

Kenneggy Sand 44

Praa Sands 44

Porthcew 43

❗ Porthleven 42
Porthleven Sands - North 42
Porthleven Sands - South 41

Mullion 41

St Ives
Penzance
St Just
Lands End
Mounts Bay
Godrevy
St Agne
Porthtow
Portreath
Redruth
Camborne
Falmouth
Helston
Mullion
Lizard P●

MULLION

Take A3283 S from Helston. R on B3296 signed Mullion. Through village to beach.

A straight west swell hits the spot here, and the more common northwest needs to be very big to make it round Lands End. Mullion might not always be the best shape, but it's more likely to have a wave than many south coast breaks and if the banks are right and winds are northeast to southeast you might get a great session here. Beware shore dump on those rare big days. Just north are 2 coves; Poldhu and Church, that may be worth a check.

PORTHLEVEN SANDS - SOUTH

A394 south from Helston, then A3083. Turn off right for Gunwalloe and keep on through to the beach.

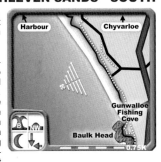

If you've come on the pilgrimage to Porthleven to find it's too small, this could be your salvation...maybe. The shore break here is among the worst in Cornwall and more often than not you will find a shapeless spine-busting dump. The pebbly Gunwalloe end sucks up most swell but high tide ain't too good. Uncrowded as spread out. Currents. Close-outs. All levels unless big.

PORTHLEVEN SANDS - NORTH

From Helston side, Head towards the town of Porthleven on Porthleven Rd, but keep going straight instead of the right turn into town.

Shore-break for crazy folk most of the time, and spine-snapping at that. Its a rocky spot with no beach left at high tide, when swells slam up against the bluff. Low tide best. Advanced. Generally a desperation spot when not much is happening at Porthleven proper. There is however, the **Pier** which breaks left and right near the harbour's southern wall.

PORTHLEVEN

In Porthleven, to west side of harbour. Follow road up the hill to cliff top; park nicely. Scrabble down path on west side of harbour mouth, channel on right.

Fickle, splendid wave. Known for it's hollow rights over a flat rock shelf, it gets sucky at low to mid tide, when pretty square barrels are possible. Higher tides are OK too but dead high is often rippy, back-washed and fat. Needs very big west, or solid / big southwest swell. 3-10ft plus. Advanced. Crowded if its ever on in summer. Can get awesome.

PORTHCEW

Head west from Helston on A394 and take left at Ashton, down Rinsey Lane. It's just past Rinsey. Alternatively, next little spot south from Praa.

Tiny little cove that does not give up its secrets easily, and is covered at high tide. Rocks at either end can form nice banks. This is a rare spot that you have to catch just right or you will leave disappointed.

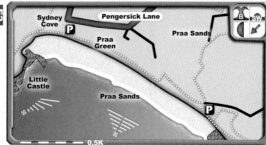

Signposts off the A394 between Helston and Perranuthnoe. Pretty, but semi-consistent beach-break best at mid tide on big SW swells. Plenty of room. East end more consistent, but still rare. Sydney cove end can have a good wave off the rocks.

KENNEGGY SAND

The next little beach a half mile west from Praa.

You need a solid SW swell and low to mid tide if you are to have a chance at catching this spot working. Cudden Head protects it from swell and some west winds, so it'll always be smaller than Perranuthnoe next door. If the that spot's onshore and big, then have a look here. Beginners, although all rocks at high tide.

PERRANUTHNOE

Head east out of Marazion to the 394. A half mile after this turn right at Perranuthnoe sign. All the way to the beach.

Rare beach-break for days when massive west swells are closing out everywhere, or a long awaited big southwest swell is getting in. Low to mid tide is the only chance, with no beach left at high. 1-4ft. Beginners. Awesome scenery is the consolation. The lucky few will get a nice right in the right corner if there's a major swell and west to nor west winds.

PORTHCURNO

From Penzance take A30 west. Turn off left for St Buryan on the B3283. Turn off and park, take tracks.

One of the most beautiful places in the world. You won't always find waves here in the white sand coves running east from the stunning Minack Theatre, but if you score it'll be less crowded than most areas. On solid west swells or a rare SW, with any north wind, there are beach-break peaks right across the stretch. Low tide only or all shore-dump. 1-6ft. All levels.

SENNEN COVE

Take the A30 west and turn off at Sennen Cove sign. Big car parks at the beach.

Consistent beach-break with spread-out peaks along the lengthy strand. If it's flat here then all else is doomed. Not ruined by the SW sea-breezes due to cliffs, but maxes out around the 6 ft mark. Most tides OK but avoid dead-high. Middle tides with 3-5ft NW swell is best, and barrels if wind has east in it. Staple diet for St Ives Surfers. Busy in summer but manageable. Other times of year no problem. All levels.

Blue Lagoon all inclusive surf holidays at Sennen 01736 871817

GWYNVER

Just north from Sennen Cove. Drive back up the A30 and take a left past Escalls to the carpark.

The most consistent surf in Cornwall, taking any direction from south through northwest. Gwynver is a beautiful beach-break that can get hollow if the banks are right, and has a patchy sand & rock point at northern end. All too often though, it's a mush-fest, and high tide can be unsurfably fat. 2-6ft. All levels unless big. Currents. Crowds OK.

PORTHMEOR

E2

In St Ives, the beach is well signed and there's a car park by the Tate Modern. Quality beach-break when exposed beaches are huge and wind is south or even southwest. It's a life-saver during stormy weather, but small unless there's a solid swell. Any tide is OK but dead high can be too fat. If very large, paddle round to **Foxholes**; a fun left-hander over shingle. You can walk there but this involves minor dicing with low cliffs.

Semi-consistent. 1-8ft plus. All levels. Crowded.

St Ives Backpackers central town location 01736 799444

CARBIS BAY

Sign posted on the way to Lelant from St Ives.

More of a kids beach than a surf spot, but if there's enough swell it can work. Any tide can be OK but dead low is mushy as can be. Off-shore in a SW wind, and good ice cream is not far away. Beginners, except rare big winter days. Fickle. Uncrowded except summer. 1-5ft, occasionally more. The story does not

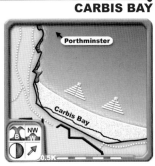

end here, as you might stumble across a quality lesser-known spot towards Porthminster involving a climb and a jump off the rocks. We have removed this spot from the guide to encourage you to use initiative, and avoid the author being vilified by all at the Sloop. 47

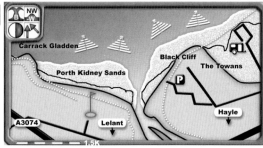

Head into Hayle village from St Ives and follow signs to The Towans. Huge tidal range makes sandbanks unpredictable. Best at mid tide on a solid 3-5ft W swell, & SE winds. Crowds no problem due to length, but sailboarders may hit you! Further up towards Gwithian can be more consistent, but more affected by the wind. Long walk. 1-6ft. Quite consistent. All levels. Currents. Ask a local where Philps Bakery is, to experience the best pasty ever.

GWITHIAN

N from Hayle on B3301. Several sandy paths on left to beach carparks before Gwithian village itself. Long beach absorbs crowds well. Further north you go the more size but often the more wind if it's SW. Some of the most consistent banks can be found at **Red River**, the rivermouth area before Godrevy, which can get the lions share of swell…and wind! Always bigger than Porthmeor. All levels. Consistent. Currents.

48

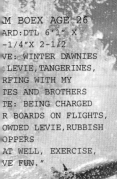

M BOEX AGE 26
ARD:DTL 6'1" X
-1/4"X 2-1/2
VE: WINTER DAWNIES
LEVIE,TANGERINES,
RFING WITH MY
TES AND BROTHERS
TE: BEING CHARGED
R BOARDS ON FLIGHTS,
OWDED LEVIE,RUBBISH
OPPERS
AT WELL, EXERCISE,
VE FUN."

BOARDRIDERS - HAYLE - CORNWALL
THE HARDWARE SPECIALIST
DOWN THE LINE SURFCO.
MARKET SQUARE ARCADE,COPPERHOUSE, HAYLE
TR274EA T:01736757025 F:01209832080

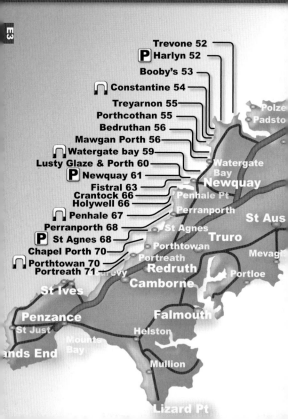

E3: CORNWALL MID NORTH

E3

Trevone 52
Harlyn 52
Booby's 53
Constantine 54
Treyarnon 55
Porthcothan 55
Bedruthan 56
Mawgan Porth 56
Watergate bay 59
Lusty Glaze & Porth 60
Newquay 61
Fistral 63
Crantock 66
Holywell 66
Penhale 67
Perranporth 68
St Agnes 68
Chapel Porth 70
Porthtowan 70
Portreath 71

Polze
Padsto
Watergate Bay
Newquay
Penhale Pt
Perranporth
St Agnes
St Aus
Truro
Porthtowan
Portreath
Redruth
Camborne
Mevagi
Portloe
St Ives
Falmouth
Penzance
St Just
Helston
Mounts Bay
nds End
Mullion
Lizard Pt

TREVONE

From Padstow west on the B3276, take a right on Trevone Rd before Harlyn.

Rarely working, but when on (solid WNW swell, SE winds), there's a quality right (low tide) and left (mid tide) here over sand bottom. The east side of the beach has a nice rip that hugs the rocks, and conveyors you out on the bigger days. Winter spot. Out of the way. 2-6ft. Advanced. Very fickle. Tight local crew protect the spot so be quiet and respectful. If you had to cross the Camel Bridge to get here, do not miss Barnecutts Pasties in Wadebridge.

HARLYN

West on the B3276 from Padstow. Turn right (sign) before St Merryn. Carpark before bridge on right.

Your saviour when it's huge and windy, Harlyn offers protection from SW storm winds, and is often hollow and peaky when everywhere else is a froth-fight. Low tide means close-outs, with mid best and high rippy and bumpy, but there can be good power here compared to other spots. E end usually bigger. Hollow. Crowded (more so every year), but many peaks. 2-6ft. All levels. Advanced when big. Inconsistent.

52

BOOBY'S

Hike up from Constantine, or drive in from Harlyn taking a right before Constantine, then down to the end of the dirt track. Hoof across the field.

Booby's Bay

Constantine

0.75K

Low tide break providing good hollow shape, but usually unrideable at high tide. Can provide the odd barrel on easterly wind and solid WNW swell in winter. Solid local crew so getting waves involves patience.

2-8ft. Intermediate to advanced. Quality spot. Pretty consistent but tide must be right.

Secret Southwest / Pete Adams

CONSTANTINE

Next to Boobys. Signs from Padstow and stay south of golf course.

Reliable beach-break with outside sets good at low tide on big days, & peaky, more powerful peaks in the middle at high tide. **The Point** (N end) can be good if the golf club's stream is flowing and sculpting the sand. **The Reef** (S end) will work if you're V lucky, on spring high tide. 2-8ft. Advanced when big. Crowds in summer. Margaret Thatchers favourite spot (for walking).

TREYARNON

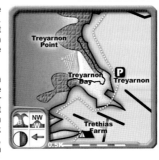

Its right next door to the south of Constantine. From Padstow, head west on the B3276 past Harlyn and Constantine Bay. Take a right at Treyarnon Farm.

Another small beach with sand peaks and a possible right in the bottom corner off the rocks. Fickle spot that disappears at high tide, you need a bit of luck to get it right. Constantine, next door, is better known and more consistent. 2-6ft. Surprisingly crowded if on. All levels.

PORTHCOTHAN

On the B3276 coast road north from Newquay, after Mawgan Porth.

Out of the way, this little bay will produce some good hollow beach-break peaks if the banks are right. A small stream is the main factor here; when the flow combines with the swell to direct the sand-banks into the right shape then you will get barrelling lefts and rights on low to mid tide. Too high, and the beach is gone. 1-6ft. Fickle. Uncrowded. All levels. Nice rip can form to get you out the back.

BEDRUTHAN STEPS

North from Mawgan Porth on the B3276. Just past village of Bedruthan. Look for Bedruthan Steps signs.

Beach-break peaks abound, and it is no loss if you've checked it and all is flat (in this case everywhere will be flat anyway). This area gets marmalized by any wind with west in it, and closed out on those very big winter swells unless an off-shore wind is there to comb it. Low tide best. Awful paddle-out. Not far north, you will find some peeling little gems if the tides are higher on a solid northwest swell and easterly wind. 1-8ft. All levels.

MAWGAN PORTH

Off the B3276 north from Newquay, after Watergate and the village of Trevarrian.

Exposed beach-break open to the winds but also any available swell. Stream flow sculpts banks and after a big outflow or major rain this can get very good. Best on a middling tide; High gets fatter but wind protected, low can slow it up, especially on a big spring tide. It's not one of the most surfed beaches around so crowds are manageable. A bit of a trip to get there. 1-6ft. All levels.

KITESURFING THE SOUTHWEST

If wind and wave combinations are not perfect for surfing, the West Country offers a pretty extreme alternative. Andreya Wharry shares some of the primo locations.

Watergate Bay: Loads of space but at low tide ONLY! Works in any wind with west in it with straight west best. Watergate can deal up some big heavy waves so it never gets boring.

Gwythian, The Bluff: A great river mouth. On a big swell it can send ramps running up the channel... fun! It works on winds with North in them except NE, and at most tide states but not a spring high as this only leaves a little bit of beach. On a small neap tide with no swell you can sometimes get away with it. Can also be great with tide against wind as on a light summer day you can steal a couple of extra knots.

Daymer Bay: SE or NW winds running up or down the Camel estuary. Can be great with a 6knt current, as in the summer you can sail in very light winds. Conversely, when wind & tide are in the same direction, it's impossible to stay up wind and you can get spat out to sea! Mid tide is best, low tide is poss but there's not much of channel. Also on high tide there's no beach, and a huge wind shadow if wind is SE.

Isles of Scilly: More of a holiday destination this one as there's a short boat or plane trip involved. Tropical looking clear waters, island hopping possible with a boat, and all wind directions covered. Frequent helicopter landings on Tresco; check the times and land your kite.

Andreya Wharry / Christian Black

**At Watergate Bay we have
everything you need to surf:**
* A spectacular beach break
* Surf board test centre
* BSA surf school
* Surf rental
* The Beach Hut Bistro and Bar
* The Extreme Store

Watergate Bay, it's not a
thing, or a product to buy,
or a place to sit or ever
something to learn

... it's a way of life!

www.watergatebay.co.uk
01637 860840

Head north about 2 miles from Newquay on the B3276. There's a carpark before the beach path on your left, just before the road splits to the right. You can also take the left fork up the hill to check the coastline.

Consistent all-year round beach-break, that sometimes produces power waves and the odd barrel. It will pick up any swell going, and works through all tides. Mid tide with south-east winds and a 3-5ft ground-swell is best, and fast peaky take-offs result. Bigger swells are sometimes a little messy here, and west winds are onshore. On higher tides the south end is cleaner on the prevailing southwesterlies but the bay is split. Busy in summer as there is major camping and carpark here, but the many peaks spread the load and its a good place to be anyway. If its flat here it will be flat almost everywhere.

1-6ft. Can handle more if a nice offshore breeze combines with long-period swell. All levels although advanced when over 4ft. Currents when sizey. Autumn & winter best.

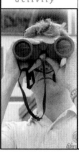
PORTH & LUSTY GLAZE

Head for Lusty Glaze road at the east end of town, and park in the back streets. 2 cliff paths/steps.

Semi consistent beach-break working through the tides, and with a slight degree of protection from the winds. If it's on, you will see the lines from the cliff-top. Generally less populated then Tolcarne, and Lusty Glaze is joined to it at low tide. High tide swallows both beaches up.

Matt's Surf Lodge central-bar-p/king £8+b&b 01637874651
surflodge.co.uk

NEWQUAY'S TOWN BEACHES

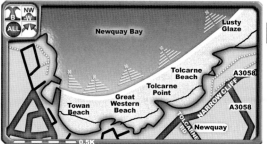

In Newquay, you'll glimpse them beneath the cliffs from the coast road: along with other surfers who stop illegally in front of the guest houses and run across the road to check the surf.

On a winter's day with huge swell running and a nasty SW gale, the town beaches are probably your best bet. From **Lusty Glaze** in the east, through to the **Harbour** in the west, these beaches filter out swell and wind incrementally, to produce some good shape and the odd small barrel if right. **Towan**, the western-most beach, is the most protected from storm southwest winds, and holds the best shape if it is huge, especially the lefts near harbour wall. It is the least consistent though. **Great Western** and **Tolcarne** are a little more reliable, and a bit less protected from the winds. Both can hold good hollow, fast, lined up peaks on a middle tide if there's solid swell. At low tide the four beaches become one long strip. In summer; a nightmare and rarely worth surfing. This is a winter or late autumn spot. Major power swells are needed to make it around Towan Head. 1-10 ft. Crowded as hell. Parking a challenge in summer - check the back streets. Avoid on bank holiday weekends unless you have ulterior motives or like antiquated German vehicle engineering.

Newquay Backpackers very near to town & beaches 01637 123456
The Zone overlooking world famous Fistral beach 01637 123456

ØCEAN✴MAGIC

surfer - dave young   photo - kirsten prisk

www.oceanmagicsurfboards.com
oceanmagic@btconnect.com

Signs in the town of Newquay, huge carpark on the beach.

The most famous surfing beach in Europe. Whilst reef breaks and some coves may get better waves, the probability of getting good waves on any given day of the year is higher here than just about anywhere.

South Fistral works  through all tides, with good lefts and some rights. It is a bit more protected on bigger days with a southwest wind. **North Fistral** is often bigger, & gets hollow at low tide, especially off the rocks at the top end, where there's usually one of the best left and right peaks. **Little Fistral**, right around the corner and almost swallowed up at high tide, can have great shape too on low to mid. Autumn swells from NW-W are best but it is consistent all year round. 1-8ft. Intermediate +. Crowds in the summer and plenty of room in winter.

The Cribber, out the back of Towan Head off Cribber Rock, is a fickle off-shore reef for hell-men, although it rarely breaks in a rideable way. It needs a very big groundswell in the 8-12ft range to show, and perfect south-east offshore breeze to hold shape. In these conditions it'll hold any size.

Newquay Backpackers very near to town & beaches
01637 879366

The Zone overlooking world famous Fistral beach 01637 872089

SURFERS PARADISE

newquay cornwall england

64 tower road, newquay, tr7 1ly   01637 877373

BOARDS, WETSUITS & ACCESSORIES
EVERYTHING THE HARDCORE SURFER NEEDS

We have hundreds of boards in stock for you to choose from...

NIGEL SEMMENS, PLEASURE STIX, LOST, DHD, JS, NEV, MAURICE COLE, AL MERRICK, SURFTECH, BEAR, MCTAVISH, CHOPS LASCELLES and more...

...SHORTBOARDS, FISH, DOUBLE ENDERS, FUNBOARDS, SLIPPERS, MINIMALS, LONGBOARDS, RETRO SINGLE FINS AND TWIN FINS...

...and, if you cant find exactly what you want, then with the helpful advice of our highly trained staff, we have a
FULL CUSTOM ORDER SERVICE,
with over 30 years of shaping experience!

What Else?
Not only do we stock a wide range of *RIPCURL* wetsuits and accessories, *C-SKINS* accessories, and a huge range of leashes deck pads, boardbags, wax, *FCS* fins, dvds... but we've also got all the *HIRE EQUIPMENT* you need - from wetsuits to bodyboards to custom surfboards. Great access and you can even park outside the shop!

 SURFERS PARADISE IS YOUR ONE STOP BOARD SHOP!

Fistral firing / Jim Michell / barefootmedia.co.uk

Just west of Newquay, follow signs to carpark.

At low to mid tide, this is
a huge stretch and a long
walk to the water. The river is responsible for some
good banks if you catch it
right, but it needs a bit of
size to get in; Fistral is usually a lot bigger, especially
on higher tides when this
spot retreats into its shell.
Protected from SW winds.
Often a good peak in the
west corner out of the wind
too. 1-6ft. All levels. Less crowded than the other Newquay spots.

Revolver: your one stop service for retro glide 01637 873962

Head south from Newquay
on the A3075. A mile after
Crantock take a right and
follow signs. Trek across
sand dunes.

A less surfed spot that can
get good. The stream in the
middle can help give shape
to the banks, creating well
formed beach-break peaks
on occasion. A lot of beach
is swallowed up at high tide
so low-mid can be best. 1-
6ft. Uncrowded. All levels.
Consistent. If not always
good quality.

PENHALE CORNER

At the northern end of Per-ran Sands. Sniff your way from Perranporth via Per-ran Sands Caravan Park and take the dune track.

A solid swell magnet with a wide array of beach-break peaks down towards Per-ranporth. Quality rights can line up well off Ligger Point, where it can get crowded if good. Beach peaks tend to have a bit more power than Perranporth, and are better on middle tides, just before the beach disappears. Best in the morning as wind-affected. Plenty of room except the point. All levels. 2-8ft.

St Agnes Winter / Jim Michell

PERRANPORTH

Well signed off the A30.

So many options, but the most well known corner is in town off **Droskyn Point**, where sandbars can hold good shape to about 6-8ft. This section is also a little more protected from prevailing SW winds. Any tide OK, but low can be more sluggish depending on banks. Further up the beach are miles of peaks that can absorb most

crowds; a good spot to check in summer. Generally gets more windy, less crowded, and bigger the further up you go. Summer is a bit of a mad-house although this is a great fun part of Cornwall to be in at that time. 1-6ft. All levels. Consistent. Crowds OK.

ST AGNES

Off the A30 on the B3285. From the village, take Quay Rd to car-park. Parking very tight.

A spot to head for when it's big and blown out on the west-facing beaches, but beware crowds and parking hassles. Aggie has protection from SW winds, and filters larger swells into clean powerful peaks over sand and pebble bottom. Rights dominate. Because it is one of the only spots in

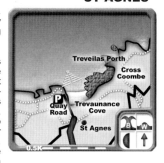

these conditions, and is quite compact, expect healthy competition for your wave and be a little patient. Fickle. Some rocks. Tight local crew may not welcome you. Advanced unless small. 2-8ft.

CHAPEL PORTH

Off the A30 Take the B3277 to St Agnes, and go left before you get there, on Goonvrea rd. Park at the end.

Banks here are sculpted by a small stream, so there can be better shape than anywhere on the right day. On a solid 3-6ft west or northwest swell, and south to east winds you can get powerful peaks and barrels here, especially on the middle tides. Summer sea breezes badly affect the wave so surf it early or look at your little cockerel on the roof. There are a number of peaks - just as well, as it gets pretty busy except in the dead of winter. 1-8ft. Consistent.

PORTHTOWAN

A few miles north of Cambourne on the A30, signs for Porthtowan on B3277.

Extensive stretch of sand in tin mining country, that pulls some of the more powerful surf in the area. Any tide is good, with the beach steepening up at high. Likes ESE winds ideally, with south-westerlies being cross-shore and not too horrid if you're surfing the southern corner. Intermediates. Summer numbers can be pretty hectic although it is out of the way. 1-8ft plus. Consistent.

Coming into Portreath on the B3300, follow signs to beach.

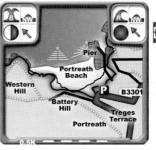

There's a good quality all-tide beach-break here, and it can get hollow on most south winds with decent swell. The west corner is protected from the southwest winds that plague some of the main spots round here. If it's big enough, a wedgy hollow, fast right can break off the **Harbour Wall** on higher tides. This spot gets crowded, and invaded by body-boarders. 1-8ft. Semi consistent. Intermediate plus. Rocks at east end.

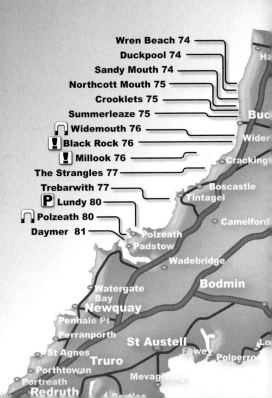

E4: CORNWALL NORTH

Wren Beach 74
Duckpool 74
Sandy Mouth 74
Northcott Mouth 75
Crooklets 75
Summerleaze 75
Widemouth 76
Black Rock 76
Millook 76
The Strangles 77
Trebarwith 77
Lundy 80
Polzeath 80
Daymer 81

Bude
Wider
Crackingt
Boscastle
Tintagel
Camelford
Polzeath
Padstow
Wadebridge
Bodmin
Watergate Bay
Newquay
Penhale Pt
Perranporth
St Austell
St Agnes
Truro
Fowey
Polperro
Porthtowan
Portreath
Mevagis
Redruth

From Bude town, Sandy Mouth is signed north, and Duckpool is just up the road from there. Best access is via Stibb.

Sandy Mouth: Expansive beach-break with multiple left and right peaks. Most tides are OK here, and the shape varies with the banks. 2-5ft northwest - west swell and an easterly wind are best. Consistent. All levels. Can be busy in summer.

Duckpool: Small cove with beach-break peaks and a right-hander in the top corner, breaking into the cove. 2-6ft plus. Inconsistent. Can get crowded but also can be quality. All levels.

Wren Beach: Another fickle little cove with low tide peaks over sandy bottom. All levels, rarely too crowded.

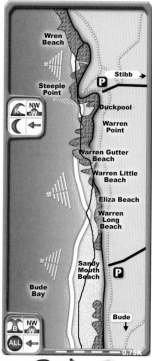

Head into Bude, well signed off the 3072.

Summerleaze, at the south end of the beach, is the centre of the action and a busy beach-break. It works well on lower tides and is generally pretty approachable. On higher tides when there's swell, rights and lefts can work on either side, in towards the harbour off the rocks. 1-8ft. All levels. Semi consistent.

Crooklets has quality beach-break in the middle, and the rocks at either end hold some good shape too. On higher tides a pitching little right can form just up from the pool. Wrangles Rocks can also throw up a nice low tide right. 2-6ft. Intermediate plus. Consistent. You can stroll up from here and pick your beach-peak on lower tides.

Northcott Mouth, further north, can be a good bet for less crowds and quality low tide banks. Disappears at high tide. 1-6ft. Intermediate plus. Consistent.

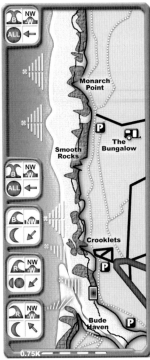

There are a few semi-secret spots both north and south of Bude that have been removed or omitted so that you can go and explore for yourself.

75

WIDEMOUTH & BLACK ROCK

Widemouth is very well signed, and Black Rock is at the southern end.

The beach-break is one of the more mellow experiences, with gently mushing waves over an expanse of dark sand. Beginners. Summer crowds. Consistent. **Black Rock** in the south however, is a powerful set-up over patchy rock. There can be a jacked up take-off zone, and some hollow fast waves on a middle to

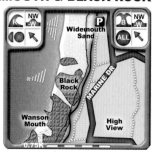

high tide and solid NW winter swells. Holds more size than most, up to 10ft plus. Experts only. **Wanson Mouth** just south also gets heavy and good.

MILLOOK

Near Widemouth. If you have time to burn, sniff it out. Heavy winter left-hand point over slab, boulder and shingle, that requires huge swell to even break. Paddle-out is between rocks and there is a real risk of dents to board and body. This spot has exposed rocks, unimpressed locals, heavy non-locals, boils, barrels, current, and an awful paddle-in if things go wrong and you have to swim for it. All this in a spot

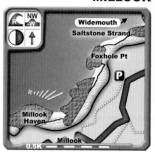

that is unsurfable in all but the rarest of tide/swell combinations. 3-10ft. No parking. 10 years ago this was a mysto spot... these days it's a worst kept secret with the crowds to match. Avoid, and never take a crowd.

THE STRANGLES

Follow the coast rd south out of Crackington Haven. The Strangles is just out of the village, beneath the cliffs.

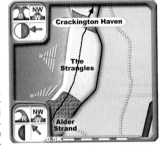

Exposed beach-break with OK shape depending on banks, & working on lower tides. An occasional left-hander in the corner can reel across a rock and sand bottom, and is slightly less damaged by the southwest winds. A beautiful spot if not always blessed with quality surf. At high tide it is a rock field so avoid. Just north, **Crackington Haven** itself hosts a low-tide rock shelf & beach-break that's worth a check on bigger days or during southwest winds.

TREBARWITH

From Delabole; take B3314 N, then Trebarwith Rd a mile on left. Major carpark at beach.

Scenic spot that almost disappears at high tide, when rock-dodging becomes an essential art. Can form quality beachbreak peaks on low to mid, with bigger swells breaking right out towards the island. Relatively powerful for this area. Needs E winds to clean up. Intermediate plus. Crowds in summer but otherwise OK. On big swell and southwest winds, there are options north that you can check.

Somewhere North / Pete Adams

Round the corner from Polzeath and a horrendous hike in.

Hidden, inaccessible spot that takes huge winter swells and is offshore in any southerly winds. Not worth the long hike unless Polzeath is closed out. If on, good lefts and rights on sand at low tide, with beaches disappearing at high. 1-6ft. Very very fickle. All levels. Winter only.

Prepare for a bracing cliff walk, great scenery, and probable disappointment when you get to the water.

B3314 N from Wadebridge. Polzeath sign on left.

A gentle but consistent surf experience. Shallow shelving beach can beat the power out of most swell to create spilling improvers waves. Outer banks can produce nice big peaks on lower tide if swell is large. One of the more accessible and consistent waves in the area so can get busy in summer. Beginners plus. Consistent. 1-8ft.

DAYMER & THE DOOM BAR

Head into Polzeath, and up over the hill to Trebetherick. Daymer Bay is a right turn down Daymer Lane .

Rare indeed to see this lot work, but if there's a huge west - northwest swell, at low tide (spring tide best) and winds are south to east, the sandbar at the mouth of the Camel Estuary can throw up big lefts and rights. Currents are outrageous. Experts only. Boat from Rock/Padstow is the safer way. Daymer Bay hosts an even rarer right-hand point over patchy sand & rock. A bit of a pirate's tale really.

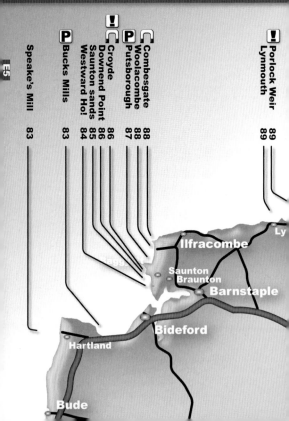

Porlock Weir 89
Lynmouth 89

Combesgate 88
Woolacombe 88
Putsborough 87

Croyde 86
Downend Point 86
Saunton sands 85
Westward Ho! 84

Bucks Mills 83

Speake's Mill 83

Ilfracombe
Saunton
Braunton
Barnstaple
Bideford
Hartland
Bude
Ly

SPEAKE'S MILL

Heavily guarded spot near Hartland Quay.

Out-of-the way mission to find this semi-consistent spot with it's tight local crew who will not be happy to see you. Essentially a reef left & right combo that breaks left or right depending on tides. There can be some hollow power on middle and low tides (when the lefts can be good). Regardless of the lore this is no Shark Island although the rock is pretty jagged. Current, and often no shape. 2-8ft plus. Advanced. Rocks on land and in the water. Some may find it overrated. Do not arrive with a group. Do not paddle straight up to the peak, Wait your turn.

BUCKS MILLS

A39 west from Bideford. Take a right at Bucks Cross toward caravan park, and follow road to end.

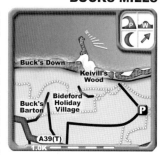

Shingly rocky entry to this extremely rare left-hander. It breaks on patchy rock in only the hugest of groundswells, preferably on dead low tide (what little beach there is disappears at high). Can get very hollow and pretty fast. Well protected from storm southwest winds, so this is a winter or late autumn spot. There is an outer bommie that works left and right if big. Very inconsistent, so not worth the effort unless you do your sums beforehand. 3-10ft. Can get crowded if word gets out. Advanced.

WESTWARD HO!

Signs from Bideford will take you the town and its various beach carparks.

Beginners beach-break paradise. This outrageously long, wide strip of sand slopes so gently that even the most power-packed winter swell is battered and bruised before it gets near breaking. The result is slow spilling stuff, perfect for learners. The main plus is the ample space and many peaks that absorb any number of surfers and other styrofoam devices ridden by kids.

Left end by the village is generally cleaner and smaller. It's slightly protected from southwesterlies.

All year round fun. Beginners. 1-4ft plus. No major hazards although there can be currents if big.

Westward Ho

GOLF LINKS RD

0.75K

SAUNTON SANDS

From Barnstaple, head to Braunton on the A361, then B 3231 to Saunton.

Enormous, sometimes gutless spot whatever the tide. Saunton is not a place to go if you want advanced conditions, but there is plenty of space for those looking for a hassle-free session. The northern corner gives a bit of protection from the northerly winds (Ralphs Reef is a rare right), but the strip is very wind-blown on the prevailing southwesterly conditions.

A fun learners spot with plenty of room to express yourself, and scant punishment for mistakes. Currents are sometimes a factor however as the tidal range is phenomenal.

This is a scenic, mellow part of the world to spend time if the surf isn't providing an alternative.

1-5ft. Beginners plus. Uncrowded except summer.

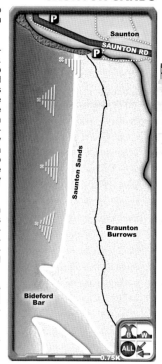

DOWNEND

Nestled in between Saunton and Croyde, is Downend Point.

The Point; a long right-hander with solid take-off, whackable mid-section and fast hollow inside. Best just before or after low, and needing solid 3ft + swell. Head here when beach maxed out. Currents. Wide sets. Paddle out from Croyde side. Advanced only. Rare inside point also, but for uber-experts only. Way out the back is a mysto reef that can work if huge, on a super-low tide: **Oyster Falls** is for hell-men/tow-in surfing, and as such has barely been tapped.

CROYDE

Most consistent, powerful beach-break in Devon. Shapely sand peaks across the bay on all tides, but low provides **much** faster, steeper walls & barrels. Peaks north of the stream are generally better. **The Reef**, at the N end, is a quality **rare** R, needing very high tides or it's a boiling rock field. Shallow sucky take-off. Needs major swell. Advanced only as errors = dents. Reef does not handle numbers so only surf it if you are with a local. Some good lefts at south end.

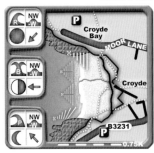

www.croyde-surf-cam.com The Pink Shop 01271 890 453
SURF SOUTH WEST Surf Schools 01271 890 400 www.surfsouthwest.com

PUTSBOROUGH

Head N from Croyde up Jones Hill. Just the other side of Baggy Point.

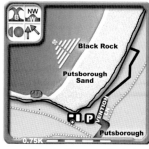

Usually an incredibly easy spot for beginners, across a never-ending beach with huge tidal range. Prevailing southwest winds are blocked or even offshore at the bottom end of the beach; a plus on a windy summer afternoon although the swell doesn't always get in here. It can get hollow and fast on a huge ground-swell with any south wind and a pushing tide; at these times, use the channel near the southern cliffs. 1-5ft. Beginners plus. Fun spot.

WOOLACOMBE

A361 S from Ilfracombe.

Expanse of super-mellow beach-break along this huge beach, working on all tides. The sand just about disappears on high tide, when the northern end gets a respectable right-hand peak. You can jump off these rocks almost straight out the back at this time. Also on higher tides, there is a good left and right just south of the stream. 1-5ft, beginners plus. Crowds are well absorbed, and its quieter than Putts or Croyde. **The Little Beach Hotel,** Esplanade, Woolacombe, 01271 870 398 info@surfersworld.co.uk

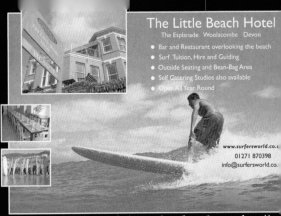
COMBESGATE

Just around the rock from North Woolacombe.

Barricane Beach, all but swallowed up at high tide, is a spot to head for when the main beach at Woolacombe is over-heated. At low tide there are faster peaks here than anywhere nearby and crowds can be slightly less. It's onshore in a southwesterly but offers protection from north winds. 2-6ft. Intermediate to advanced. Rocks at high tide, rips towards low. Medium crowds in summer, winter peaceful.

LYNMOUTH

Off the A39 on Exmoor. Awesome drive.

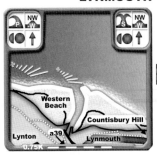

An incredibly long, but sometimes sluggish left-hand point works over pebbles and a few other obstructions. On the hugest of ground-swells however, it will deliver power, weight and thickness. You'll see it to the west of the rivermouth. Any tide is OK, and if on it will be horribly crowded. There's a couple of other peaks, notably the rivermouth left (and lesser right), which can get good and link up although again, not a power wave except on higher tides and larger swells. 1-5ft. Inconsistent. Crowded always. Scenic area.

PORLOCK WEIR

East of Lynmouth to the village. The break is opposite the car park.

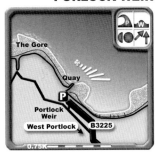

One of many spots you can head to around here when huge groundswell is running. Long, sometimes well shaped left-hander over pebbles. It rarely gets over a couple of feet here and if it does it can be crowded because other options are probably closed out. All levels. Tread carefully here, and never arrive with a group. Don't paddle straight into the peak; rather wait on the shoulder for a while, politely. Welcome to Somerset!

Hartley Reefs / Black Middens / Lewis Arnold

SURF DATA

Background

Sometimes erroneously known for its variable water quality rather than its line-ups, there is quality to be found along the length of the north and east coasts, as well as an array of scenic beaches and harbours to punctuate your surf trip. There's something the locals don't want you to know: The surf here can be awesome, there is an abundance of brilliant reef, groyne and beach-breaks, and it's off-shore a lot.

When to go

Prevailing winds are from the southwest, which is good news for this coast. However major swells can often occur during frontal conditions when winds blow in from all points of the compass. If you are lucky, a long-period Arctic Circle storm-generated swell will co-incide with the southwesterlies. **Summer**: Often flat, on-shore and crowded. You might catch an opportunistic southeast summer swell. **Autumn**: Go as late as you can and there is a good chance of a solid north swell emanating from low latitude weather systems. **Winter**: very good chance of more powerful north swells, and extremely cold water. Quality corner spots and reefs often only show on these bigger pulses. **Spring**: Water is at its coldest, some great sessions are to be had. Usually uncrowded outside public holidays and weekends. **Hazards** - Cold water. Some pollution. Check www.sas.org.uk.

M	Swell Range		Wind Pattern		Air		Sea	Crowd
	Feet	Dir'	Am	Pm	Lo	Hi		
J	0-6	n	variable	var/sw	-5	10	7	low
F	0-6	n	variable	var/sw	-5	10	6	low
M	0-5	n	variable	var/sw	3	13	7	low
A	0-5	n-ne	variable	var/sw	6	16	19	med
M	0-4	n-se	variable	var/sw	9	17	11	med
J	0-4	n-se	variable	var/sw	13	23	12	hi
J	0-3	ne-se	variable	var/sw	15	25	13	hi
A	0-3	ne-se	variable	var/sw	15	24	14	hi
S	0-6	n-se	variable	var/sw	13	24	13	med
O	0-7	n-ne	variable	var/sw	12	18	12	med
N	0-7	n-ne	variable	var/sw	8	12	10	low
D	0-7	n-ne	variable	var/sw	0	10	9	med

E6: NORTHEAST

Berwick-upon-Tweed
Holy Island
Belford
Seahouses
Beadnell Bay
Embleton
Alnwick
Alnmouth
Ellington
Newbiggin
Morpeth
Blyth
Seaton Sluice
Whitley Bay
Tynemouth
Newcastle
Whitburn
Gateshead
Sunderland
Chester Le Street
Seaham
Singleton
Durham
Peterlee

Holy Island 93
Bamburgh 93
Seahouses 94
Beadnell 94
Aln Estuary 94
Druridge Bay 94
Creswell 94
Snab Point 94
Newbiggin Point 94
Wansbeck Est' 95
Blyth 95
Hartley Reef 96
Longsands 96
Eddies 97
Black Middens 97
Whitburn Reef 98
Whitburn Sands 98
South Bents 98
Seaburn 98

HOLY ISLAND (LINDISFARNE)

S from Berwick/N from Alnwick on A1. Check tides, as the causeway is submerged mid to high. Chill in the hotel/B&Bs or harsh free camping in winter.

Loads of unsurfed reefs & points & mythical L on the S coast of the island that can handle double overhead, attract travelling soul surfers & NE locals sick of crowds. Likes big N swells. Try the local brew, Lindisfarne mead, to warm yourself up.

BAMBURGH

S from Berwick/N from Alnwick on A1. Turn off on the B1340 or B1341 into the village. Park in the dunes carpark above the beach, N of the castle.

Dramatic setting for heaps of good peaks set against castles, ruins, dolphins & seal colonies. Rocky. Big rips in big conditions. Picks up a lot of swell. Crystal clear water. Mystical place. Intermediate upwards.

A1 N from Newcastle through Alnwick. B1341 then B1340 S.

Tourist/fishing town famous for kippers and seabirds. Rarely-surfed, clean water beach/reef breaks. Good waves in most swell conditions. Currents. When winds have N in them, a trip S past the harbour towards **Beadnell** can yield interesting reef and beach options. Further on, **Low Newton, Embleton, Craster** and **Longhoughton** merit exploration. Next up, **Boulmer** has epic hollow stuff. The **Aln Estuary** at Alnmouth can offer some good sandbar peaks on any swell if the wind is SW to NW.

From Newcastle, take the A188/189 N to Newbiggin. The Point is out past the church (which gives it its alternative name) and lifeboat station.

Clean water, rarely surfed, Big wave R reef break that suits the adventurous or advanced surfers. Shallow, rocky and rippy. Adventurers head N along the coast for more possible options around Ellington (**Snab Pt**) and **Creswell** (The Scars and the Beach both host hollow goods). At the top end of **Druridge Bay**, Hadston Carrs by Low Hauxley, is worth a look.

From Newcastle, take the A188/189 N. Turn off on the A193 to Blyth. Go through town and turn L at the Newsham round-about and park up near the chippy.

The popular beach offers shelter on big blown out N swells & can get fast & quite heavy. Various peaks on sand or pebble bottom. Likes a NW swell and any east wind although rare south swells are good by the pier, which offers protection from northerly winds.

The southern, **Seaton Sluice** end by Sandy Island is perfect sand bottom action in southwest winds, and protected from the southerly. A creek here can add to the shape of the banks so it can often be worth a look for beach-break quality.

Back up towards Newbiggin, where the 189 bridges the **Wansbeck Estuary**, you can check to you right for a tidal, polluted rivermouth set-up which can work in any available swell in west winds.

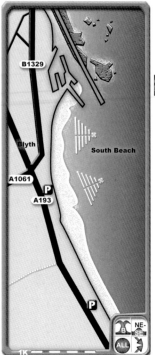

E6

B1329

Blyth

South Beach

A1061

P

A193

P

NE-SE

ALL

1K

HARTLEY REEF

Head N through Whitley Bay towards Blyth along the A193. R at the roundabout by the Delaval Arms. Park at the carpark and take the steps down the cliff.

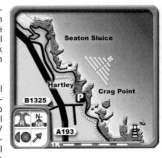

This fickle but powerful reef break can be awesome when it's on, so during a lined up swell it's well worth a check. V shallow takeoff. If it's working, jacks up and gets well overhead. One peak, so easily crowded. Advanced spot. Psycho unsurfed reefs near the lighthouse, and the point off the south end of **Seaton Sluice** beach (top of map) witnesses a mythical outer bommie.

TYNEMOUTH LONGSANDS

In Tynemouth turn down the ramp in front of the Grand Hotel. Use the rip by the old outdoor pool on bigger days.

Bustling, crowded but mellow beach break. Easily blown out, but with good off-shores this contest venue can get epic. The most reliable spot around, has a surf shop and is the local break of several UK pros. Apres surf at the Turks Head. Get up early or deal with crowds. Nice occasional point-break in this area as well.

EDDIE'S, TYNEMOUTH

In Tynemouth, this break is a small cove tucked beneath the ruins of the Priory, just N of the harbour. Park up near the Turks Head pub.

E6

This low tide spot has a central beach break, breaking on shifting sandbars & rocks, & point breaks either side. On a small swell the shore dump can be the best option. Ask around for **Pebblies.** Core locals, polluted & rippy in big conditions. Intermediate.

THE BLACK MIDDENS

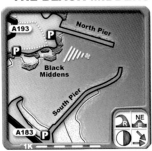

From Newcastle, take the A19 or A193 to Tynemouth, turn R in front of the Priory to the end. Walk over the hill & get in off the rocks.

Legendary heavy barrelling L reef breaking on boulder bottom in big swells. V rarely works. Powerful & unforgiving! One of the UK's best waves & site of many shipwrecks before the piers built at the Tyne mouth. Check out the plaque (& pollution!). Advanced.

WHITBURN REEFS, TYNESIDE

N end of Whitburn Bay off the A183 from Sunderland along a cliff path which has restricted access as it crosses a firing range.

A series of quality lefts breaking on rock bottom await the more intrepid surfer. All can handle overhead, but are not often surfed due to their unreliable nature, the walk in, and military restrictions. Advanced surfers breaks. To see if they are working, you need to take the stroll.

Whitburn Sands just south has some more reliable, easy beach-break options. **South Bents** is a good bet on any swell with east in it, and north to west winds. High tide covers the beach so low to mid is a safer option.

South from here is **Seaburn**, which is perfectly off-shore in a southwest wind. It can have a wave on any swell going.

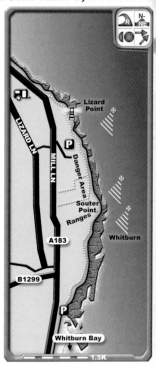

Hartlepool 100
epool — The Gare 100 !
Coatham / Redcar Scars 101 ∩
dcar — Saltburn / Penny Hole 101
tburn — Skinningrove 102
the -sea — Loftus
iles — Runswick Bay 102 ! P
ough — Whitby — Caves / Sandsend 103

Ravenscar

Scarboro N Bay 104 ∩
Scarborough — Scarboro S Bay 104
Cayton Bay 105 ☆ P
Filey — Filey Bay 106
Primrose Val 107
Bridlington — Bridlington 106

York

Hornsea
Mappleton

Kingston-upon-hull — Withernsea
Holmpton — Withernsea 107

Scunthorpe — Grimsby

HARTLEPOOL

From Middlesborough, take A178 N through Seaton Carew. (Check the many breaks on the way, all sheltered from NW winds). Park in the Old Town.

This stretch catches SE swell better than most nearby & has many beach/reef breaks on sand and rock bottoms so uncrowded waves common. There's surprising consistency round here. Something for all standards.

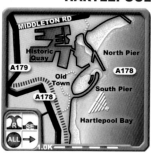

THE GARE

Inside the South Gare (breakwall) of the River Tees. A66 north from Redcar through Coatham.

World class on it's day, (a rarity) if conditions work it's a fast, heavy, polluted, near mirror-image of the **Black Middens**, breaking off a pile of cobblestones out in the river exit. Needs a major North Sea storm swell. Rumours of double overhead when it works! Access, big rips, rarity & pollution make it an advanced wave.

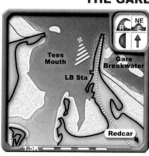

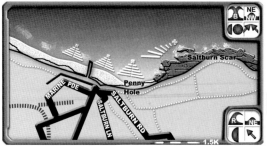

A174 from the Boro to Saltburn seafront. Park down the hill at the surf shop & pier.

Popular centre of surfing in N.Yorks. This is a fairly weak beach-break, with the better peaks focussed around the pier, which you can jump off to avoid a paddle out. They take swell from most directions, and like southwest winds. Pretty handy and there's a surf shop by the pier. As busy as you'd expect.

Heading east down the beach to the Ship Inn, on the A174, you'll find **Penny Hole**; quality beach-break left and rights (with some hollow lined up lefts often the best of the pick). Across the channel from this, under the cliffs and receiving their protection from easterly wind, is a right-hand reef/point off the **Saltburn Scar**. Expect to see it work well on south to southeast breezes and solid northeast swells. 2-8ft plus. Advanced.

Try **Coatham Sands** up past Redcar for a low power beach-break option in south winds and any east swell. On the way up, seek out the **Redcar Scars**, location of some steep but rare reef break peaks for advanced surfers.

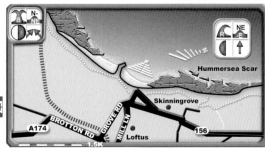

From Middlesborough, take A174 until it is Brotton Rd. Turn off L on Grove Rd for Skinningrove. Park up in the village.
Fickle but good R breaking off the Hummersea Scar on sand-covered rock at low-mid. Also 2 average beach-breaks up the beach can be found here. Pretty inconsistent spot plus suspect water quality means it's often empty in the lineup. Beginners upwards.

RUNSWICK BAY REEFS

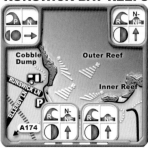

W from Whitby or E from Middlesborough on A174 Coast Rd. Park in carpark at the bottom of the hill.

Great on a massive N/NW swell. **Outer Reef** holds a huge mythical R that handles 15ft plus. **Middle Reef** is a rippy, sizey R. **Inner Reef** is a well-protected, smaller L&R reef option & **Cobbledump** is a long L breaking over rocks to the N - the only mid/high option. Often empty. All standards.

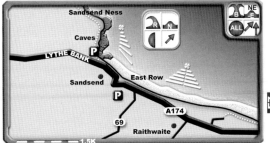

Take the A174 E from Middlesborough. Turn L N of Sandsend for the beach and Caves. Go through stone arch to carpark below cliffs. Climb over the sea wall.

Caves is a sheltered mellow long L over rocky reef. Protected from the W winds. The beach provides good, powerful, barreling A-frames at lower tides all along to Whitby Sands. Often busy & can get heavy. There are some hollow A frames to be found here on a good day. And rarely-surfed reef options to the N to be explored. Something for all. You can check the beach-break at **Whitby** just south in similar conditions.

SCARBOROUGH NORTH

Like South Bay, head for Scarborough. North Bay is well signed from the centre of town. Park on prom although it costs.

North Bay is the consistent spot for Scarborough. **Supersucks** up at the top, is a hollow, punchy reef break that you'll be lucky to catch working at its best. **The Peak** in the middle is more of a fun, consistent "A" frame. **Rights**, a right-hand shingle point under

the castle needs a solid ENE swell, when it can be a long but fun wave in south winds. It'll work on N swells in a peaky way. Plenty of rocks around. Heavy weekend crowds. Something for all.

SCARBOROUGH SOUTH

Head for Scarborough and South Bay is well signposted from the centre of town. Park on Spa and Valley roads.

Beach break "A" frames across the strip, shapely and ideal on northerly winds and huge north swells. Gets smaller as you go north. South swells tend to create close out or generate peaky little waves. There are reef rights at the south end as

well. Often busy, bodyboarders favourite, watch the rocks & backwash at high. Beach is for beginners, reef for chargers.

CAYTON BAY

3 miles S from Scarborough on A165. Turn off into grass car park at surf shop (free hot showers, nice!). Take tarmac path down.

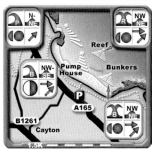

Great beach. **The Point** can be a world-class steep, hollow, pumping L. It gives some protection from northerly winds, and on a solid NE swell at high tide it is a wrapping, sucking wave with a long, carveable section. Tight take-off zone means it is well contested when on. **The Pumphouse**: Fast, sucky hollow L over sand on low tides, and a mellow L reef when tide covers the rocks...pure class. **The Bunkers**: Classic, hollow lefts and rights off a horseshoe shaped sandbar, good at mid to high. **The Reef:** Nice A-frame peak in the middle on big swell, mid to high tide. Occasional crowds but many breaks, rips (on SE swells), long paddles, & rocks!!

FILEY BAY

From York, take A64 to Scarborough. Turn R on A1039 to Filey or S on A165 from Scarbough. Well sign-posted. Park on the prom.

Fun peaky beach-breaks can be had along the length of this bay which curves round facing SE to NE, and therefore picks up all swells. Also offers protection from northerlies. Gets rippy in big conditions, but normally suitable for beginners.

Some good reefs up towards Cayton Bay merit inspection; check the cliff paths on the way there.

If swell is more south and winds are north to northwest then **Bridlington** down south has some open beach-break that can turn on the quality, and is quite consistent in summer. All levels.

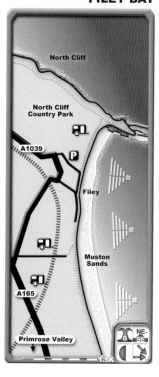

PRIMROSE VALLEY

From York, take A64 to Scarborough. Turn R on A1039 to Filey. R on A165 then after 1 mile, L at the holiday village.

The conditions need to be spot on for PV to work but it's well worth the wait (big N swell a must). When it's on it dishes out peaky A-frames that are surprisingly hollow & powerful. Definitely a high tide spot. Heavy local crowd so show respect. Intermediate / advanced break.

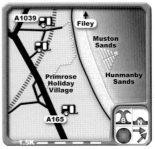

WITHERNSEA

From Leeds, take M62/A63 to Kingston Upon Hull. Follow A1033 or B1362 & B1242 from the N. Park above the beach.

Not as good as beaches N, Withernsea is the nearest break to Hull, South Yorks and the North Midlands so its shifting sandbar peaks are regularly surfed. Works on all tides but prefers a low. High tide entails dodging the groynes. Longshore rips when bigger. Crowded at weekends - if it's too much go & find **Nevills.** Further south at Maplethorpe, you'll find some well shaped beach-break among the Groynes at **Sutton-on-Sea**.

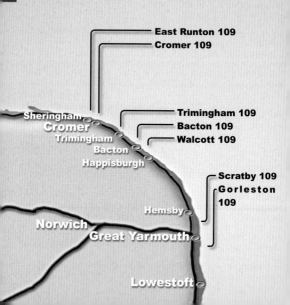

East Runton 109
Cromer 109

Trimingham 109
Bacton 109
Walcott 109

Sheringham
Cromer
Trimingham
Bacton
Happisburgh

Scratby 109
Gorleston 109

Hemsby

Norwich
Great Yarmouth

Lowestoft

EAST RUNTON

From Norwich in Norfolk, head N on A140 to Cromer, then A149 along the beach to the carpark. Take the path down the small cliffs.

Most popular break in East Anglia - L&R beach break on sand bottom. A reef offshore blocks swell at low tide, so waves are usually better N of the sewer pipe (so can get polluted). Makes it a little fickle. Heaving at weekends. Beginners upwards. Head over to **Walcott** for possible barrels on groyne-structured sand on N through E swells at low to mid tide, SW winds best. On the way you can check **Trimmingham** and **Bacton**, both can offer low tide quality.

CROMER

From Norwich, head N on A140. Cromer is well signposted. Head for the seafront & pray for a parking spot.

Exposed to N groundswells this spot has three peaks breaking over sand & pebbles. Check E side of the pier at low tide. Anglian Water has promised to tackle the serious sewage problem. V busy at weekends. Consistent. Beginner +. In the Great Yarmouth area, **Scratby** is a good bet for low-mid tide Ls on N swell, or Rs on big S-SE swell. **Gorleston** offers high tide beachbreak structured by groynes, best in W winds and solid N swell.

Hastings Wall / Remy Whiting

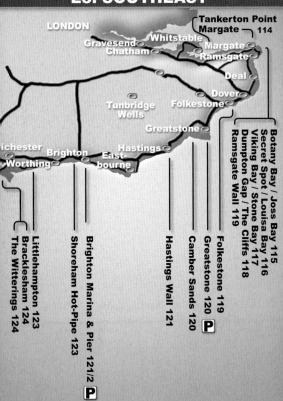

E8: SOUTHEAST

LONDON

Tankerton Point
Margate ~ 114

Whitstable

Gravesend
Chatham

Margate
Ramsgate

Deal

Dover

Tunbridge
Wells

Folkestone

Greatstone

ichester

Brighton

Hastings
East-
bourne

Worthing

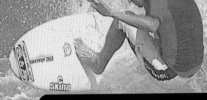

TANKERTON POINT

From M2, Junction 7 take the A299 Thanet Way towards Whitstable. At the train station, either go L to Tankerton or R to Swalecliffe caravan park and walk to the head.

A small R hand point break at the headland breaks over sandy shingle bottom. Inconsistent at best, but on a solid E swell, with offshore SW-S winds, you may find a reasonably long & mellow longboard wave.

Very good spot for learners and those new to point breaks.

MARGATE SANDS

Follow the signs on the A28 then B2015 into Margate. Park up in town near the beach.

A good fun L&R beach break, breaking on sand bottom works here on NW to NE swells - the bigger the better. Pretty consistent spot despite regularly shifting sandbars. May not be the biggest break in the world, but it's fun and there's a good scene in town too. All standards of surfers catered for. Very crowded in summer with tourists and all sorts. Stay mellow and you'll have a blast.

BOTANY BAY

From Broadstairs, take the B2052 or B2053 N to Kingsgate. Turn R and head through Kingsgate to the bay.

This is a long sandy and rocky beach with a number of L&R beach break options. At best, there are hollow peaks breaking close to shore, ideal for bodyboarders (of whom there are plenty). Pretty consistent on NW through E swells and best at mid to high tide. All standards will find something here.

E8

JOSS BAY

From Broadstairs keep going N on A2052 Stone Rd. Look for the hotel overlooking the beach.

Good L&R beach break, breaking close to shore (the Rs tend to be longer, the Ls steeper). Very fickle bars but when good, in a clean winter N/NE ground-swell at mid-high tide it is arguably better than Ramsgate. Intermediate plus break. The south end is also worth a look on SW storm swells as it'll be offshore and can get to around 2ft. Beware the obvious rocks & don't forget a lot of rubber!

SECRET SPOT

Going N into Broadstairs, take first L at top of steep hill, then private road through the estate just S of Joss Bay. Look for a smuggling tunnel, hidden by bushes, down steps to a beach.

Not a secret spot at all - funny that! This great little spot can really turn it on to produce surprisingly hollow L&Rs, that break on shallow rock bottom - so make sure you catch it at mid to high tide. Handles N and E swells, as well as big NW and W swells. Advanced break.

VIKING BAY

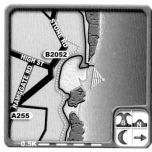

From Ramsgate, A2854 N to Broadstairs. Follow harbour road down the hill.

L&Rs on sand / rock, perfect for long mellow longboard rides if big NW & NE winter swells hit. 3 take-off points and an outside reef. The most consistent 2ft offshore waves in the Southeast, so often crowded but not really a hassle spot. All standards. **The Car Park,** right in front of the Harbour Car Park is a fast and hollow mainly R on sand. Pretty sucky when firing, possible low to mid tide barrels. Works in a variety of swells - but best in NW or N. Consistent. Good local crew.

LOUISA BAY

From Ramsgate, take the A2854 N to Broadstairs (or A255 S from Margate). Follow the harbour road down the hill to the bay.

Inconsistent but fun little L&R (mainly L) shore break, breaking on sand & rock bottom. Works consistently on all N through to E swells, better in the winter. Very tidal spot so watch out for large movements of water/currents. Mid tide only break. Intermediate plus surfers.

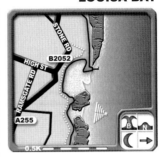

STONE BAY

Head N out of Broadstairs on A2052 Stone Rd towards N Foreland. Get to the coast and look for the 2 big E facing bays.

There's a powerful L point break, breaking at the headland on sand and chalky rock reef bottom. Best at high water. Handles plenty of swell from NW through to E swells, producing fast breaking beach breaks at mid to high tide on chalk rock and sand bottom. Exposed beach so watch out for currents. Advanced surfers breaks.

DUMPTON GAP

From Ramsgate, head to Broadstairs up the steep hill. Turn at the top & head to the cliff front. It's just N of Memorial Park, E from Dumpton Bay.

L&R beach break, breaking on sand and rock bottom. Works on N, NE through to SW and SE swells. If you catch it just right, you'll find a hollow, fast wave. Mid to high tide break only. Pretty inconsistent, but plenty of other options in the area, north and south. All standards.

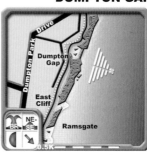

THE CLIFFS

Located just south of Dumpton Gap off the rocks.

V good little L&R barrelling shore break on sandy rock bottom, if it's working (and that is the problem). Likes a big winter SW swell and mid tide to get hollow. Hard to find, bit of a paddle out & inconsistent - so rarely any crowds. You may get it alone! Experienced surfers.

RAMSGATE WALL

From Canterbury, take the A28 E, then R on A253 to Ramsgate. Follow B2054 to the beach. Turn R & park near the East Wall.

The Wall is a wedgy R break on shallow rocky bottom off the breakwater. Do not surf it at low tide! Tight takeoff zone right next to the wall makes it a bit kamikaze (especially if big) & crowds easily. Fires on big SW swells, but picks up most swell so consistent. Advanced break.

FOLKESTONE EAST CLIFFS

Take the M20 from Ashford then A259 into Folkestone. At Dover Hill roundabout turn R on A260 then Bay Rd and park at the Tower. Walk down the cliffs.

The Reef is a hollow L&R near the harbour wall. Big paddle out in big SW swells (which it needs). Gets overhead. Advanced spot. **The Beach** works best in similar winter conditions. Beware rocks. Protected from SW winds. Check **Wear Bay** round the corner. A bit polluted but options.

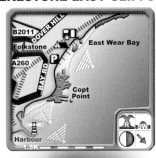

GREATSTONE-ON-SEA

From Ashford take A2070 S, then A259 L to New Romney. Follow B2071 to the beach. Park on The Parade.

If you are at Camber Sands, and a rare huge swell is pumping but on-shore southwest winds are tearing it up, check round the corner to the east at Greatstone. L&R beach break on sandy bottom. Needs North Sea storm NE, or enormous SW storm swells. High tide only break as shelves v gently. Shifting banks. Inconsistent, however, as with nearby spots, catch it right and you'll get 3ft clean longboard rides. Mellow spot for all standards.

CAMBER SANDS

From M25 J1, take M20 to Ashford. Take the A2070 S, then R on A259 to Rye. Take Camber Rd to the beach car park.

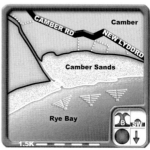

Fun, small beach-break peaks up & down this huge sandy beach, needing big SW channel storm swell (& the rarity of this combining with an offshore north westerly). A relative swell magnet compared to other spots in the area and known to get up to 6ft on occasion. Only high tide or the walk is a mission. V exposed beach with rips. They even host comps here but it is a major sailboarding/kite spot so beware the UFOs. All standards.

HASTINGS

From M25 J5, take the A21 all the way to Hastings.

Some choices in Hastings. Small R wedge to L of the breakwall off **Rock-a-Nore Pde**, E end of town, near the aquarium; good in huge SW storm, and protected from W winds. Rare! Also by the **Pier**; Mostly Rs on shingle bottom in big winter channel SW storm swell or S&SW wind chop. All V inconsistent but if you catch it just right, you'll get OK fun short rides. All standards.

fılf surf shop

3/4 west street, rottingdean, east sussex, bn27hp
01273 307465
www.filf.co.uk | filfsurfshop@btconnect.com

BRIGHTON MARINA

Take the A23 through Brighton to the seafront. Turn L on A259 or B2118 to the Marina. At the roundabout go back on yourself then take the cliff road down.

Best break in the area. L & R beachie on sandy rock bottom by the groynes, needs a big sou'west windswell 2 hours off low tide up to high tide in autumn /winter. Rarely clean but can be 3ft. Also, rare south swell rights off the marina wall can be hollow. Much talked-about local scene. Seawall is close by & can be a hazard. All standards.

121

WEST PIER, BRIGHTON

From M25 J7 take M23/A23 to Brighton. Follow signs to seafront. Park on meters between the piers.

Definitely a longboarder spot - mellow, 1-2ft but reasonably long & cruisey, breaking on sand bottom. There's a couple of other named peaks, suffering from similar fickleness of shifting banks, reliance on big S or SW ground-swell or else, wind-swell etc. Get in, get wet and take it easy. All standards.

122

SHOREHAM HOT PIPE

A259 seafront road W from Brighton to Shoreham. Turn off before the harbour on Monarch Way before the east breakwater.

L&R at hot pipe towards Southwick, breaking on sand bottom. Very popular surf spot but mellow local crew and a few other peaks about. Always best at mid-tide on good south west swell.

LITTLEHAMPTON

A27 E from Chichester or W from Brighton. Turn off on A284 then B2140 to the east pier.

Small, unreliable beach break that breaks on shifting sandbar bottom at the pier. Needs big SW ground-swell and high tide to work. Tight take-off zone makes it seem crowded with just a few people in the water. If it is good, word gets out and it will be busy. Respect the fact that there will be wave-starved crew in the water at these times. All standards.

123

BRACKLESHAM BAY

Take A3 from London to Havant. Head E on A27 to Chichester, then S on A286 and L on B2198 to the car park at the end.

More of the same as at the neighbouring Witterings. Big SW ground-swell, offshores & timing the tide right make it hard to get, but if you do strike lucky, not a bad little 3ft beach break. Lower tides best as groynes and pebbles on high are a hazardous pain, and waves shorter anyway. A friendly local crew & easy parking make it popular. All standards (especially longboarders).

E8

THE WITTERINGS

Take A3 from London to Havant. Head E on A27 to Chichester, then S on A286 and then B2179. Car parks near the beaches.

Off and on beach break, needing a strong SW storm or ground-swell & light offshores to produce anything worthy. Sandbars shift regularly although groynes can hold shape. Autumn & winter are best, when this is one of the most consistent chances of surf in the area. Crowded if it's good & a friendly local crew, based around the mecca that is the surf store. All standards. Flying sail craft abound.

124

CHANNEL SURF DATA

Background

A large population of desperate weekend surfers has charted this coastline, and continues to squeeze what little juice there is from it on weekends. Opportunistic wind swells provide relief, albeit of the messy kind, for the lucky few who stumble in during these short-lived moments. Massive west or southwest swells can penetrate The Channel on occasion to awaken reefs, beaches and the odd point. Ideally, look for a big storm out to sea west of Spain, and a high over Ireland.

When to go

Late Autumn or winter storms are the best chance of a wave anywhere on the south coast, and it is usually a question of arriving just as the winds veer or die, but before the resultant swell disappears. Long distance swell is not common unless a huge low has made it far enough south in the Atlantic, so the joy is usually brief. Most swells are quick-fire southwest wind chop that will only last as long as it's blowing on-shore.

Hazards

Pollution near urban centres, some hefty tidal currents near points and estuaries. The data chart is for the Isle of Wight. Bear in mind that east of the Island swells can decrease. Channel Islands data is found under the England Southwest section.

M	Swell Range		Wind Pattern		Air		Sea	Crowd
	Feet	Dir'	Am	Pm	Lo	Hi		
J	0-3	sw	variable	sw	0	10	8	low
F	0-3	sw	variable	sw	0	10	8	low
M	0-3	sw	variable	sw	3	13	10	low
A	0-3	sw	variable	sw	9	16	10	med
M	0-2	sw	variable	sw	9	18	13	med
J	0-2	sw	variable	sw	13	24	15	hi
J	0-2	sw	variable	sw	16	26	16	hi
A	0-2	sw	variable	sw	15	25	17	hi
S	0-3	sw	variable	sw	13	24	16	med
O	0-3	sw	variable	sw	12	18	14	med
N	0-3	sw	variable	sw	8	12	12	low
D	0-3	sw	variable	sw	0	10	10	med

E9: SOUTH

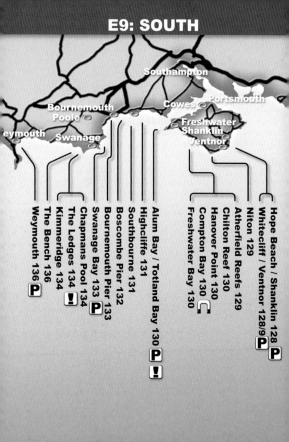

Southampton

Bournemouth
Poole

Cowes

Portsmouth

Freshwater
Shanklin
Ventnor

eymouth
Swanage

Weymouth 136 🅿

The Bench 136

Kimmeridge 134

The Ledges 134 ❗

Chapmans Pool 134 🅿

Swanage Bay 133

Bournemouth Pier 133

Boscombe Pier 132

Southbourne 131

Highcliffe 131

Alum Bay / Totland Bay 130 🅿 ❗

Freshwater Bay 130

Compton Bay 130 🚫

Hanover Point 130

Atherfield Reefs 129

Chilton Reef 130

Niton 129

Whitecliff / Ventnor 128/9 🅿

Hope Beach / Shanklin 128 🅿

Pete Adams

WHITECLIFF BAY

B3395 to Bembridge at the east tip if the island. It's on the south side of town past the school.

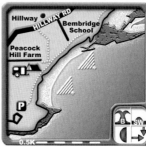

One of the better spots on the island, although it needs pretty big winter swell to get in. The good news is that when these come, accompanied as they often are by terrible southwest winds, this spot is sheltered. Mid tides are best and more powerful. 1-5ft. Crowded when on. All levels. Staple diet of Isle of Wight surfers.

SHANKLIN

From Cowes on the Isle of Wight, A3020 to Shanklin. Head to Esplanade.

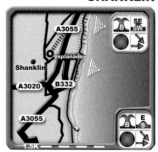

Hope Beach in the N, has good beach-break on huge SW swells. Spring highs create a wedgy rebound wave off the seawall. It needs W winds to clean it up. **The Esplanade** has some heavy , mostly right shore-dump with more ridable sets out the back further south if it is big enough. **The Groyne** here can push up wedgy Rs too. High tide best, but some off-shore limestone peaks on low if swell. Extremely rare rights further south.

VENTNOR

Isle of Wight. As for St Catherine's Point, A3020 or A3055 to Ventnor. Take the High St W through town and park up at the bay.

Potentially fast, shallow barrels over sand if a large, long period SW ground-swell gets around the island, on low tides and SW - N winds. At high tide, the shore dump is a pile-driver bodyboard wave. There's also a rare good left off the harbour wall, in east swells on high tide (and a quick dodgy right towards the sharp stuff). Rights at the west end can work on a good SW swell too. Good, uncrowded spot. Other more secluded semi secret options close by.

NITON

Southern tip of Isle of Wight. From Cowes, towards Niton on A3020 then R on A3055. Take St Catherine's Rd to the point.

The Point; A hollow R on sand & rock bottom in big SW conditions (watch out for the currents). Also a couple of L&Rs near the **Caravan Site** over sand & rock (pretty shallow at low tide). This area is off-limits, and about to be ruined by a new rock barrier. About 5 k NW up the road from here you find **Atherfield Reefs**; a left and a right working at low tide on any swell with E-N winds. Currents.

COMPTON BAY

Isle of Wight. From Freshwater Bay, Continue through on A3055 to Compton Bay and park up at the beach. **Fields**: L&Rs on sand. Best at mid-high tide, when it's got a good left-hander, but also some peaky waves at low. Crowded. Intermediates. Just S is **Hanover Point**, easy but crowded longboard spot unless a rare big SW swell hits; then it can have surprising power, good on higher tides. Rock and sand. East towards

Brook, you might notice an array of reef-breaks working on solid SW ground-swell and any N winds. Beyond this E is **Chilton Reef**; offshore left and right over rock ledge in any amount of SW swell, NE wind. Hollow on low, good on high if big enough. Advanced.

FRESHWATER BAY

Isle of Wight. From Cowes, take A3020 then A3055 thro' Yarmouth to the bay.

Low tide R point/reef break. Good & hollow if you can catch it right. Best in big winter SW ground-swells. Mid tide lines up best. High is too fat/backwashed. Rocky, and crowded if on. Currents when big. Intermediate +. Also a rare L reef here. If wind is S and swell is big

W-SW, check **Alum Bay** for low tide dumping beachie and a heavy, rarely surfed off-shore reef. Advanced only. If it really is very big **Totland Bay** has a rare left sandy point at low tide, S-E winds.

HIGHCLIFFE-ON-SEA

Take A31 S at M27 Jct1 at Southampton then A35 to Christchurch. L on A337 to Highcliffe. Take Wharncliffe Rd to the carpark.

Mainly R beachies, off the groynes on sand bottom. The further east you go, the more consistent and big it gets. SW wind-swell and low tide best. Needs light winds or easily blown out/big cross-shore currents. With a clean swell 2-3ft fun barrels. Good learner & bodyboarder spot.

SOUTHBOURNE

As for Bournemouth, follow the A338 into town. Turn off E on the Christchurch Rd. B3059 to the prom. Popular shore break around the groynes on sand & pebbles. Best in winter, when there's a little more size & a few less people. Can get quite big, peaky & hollow, but is often a fast shore-dump. Needs a SW swell and gets blown out easily. All standards.

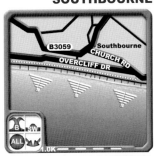

BOSCOMBE PIER

As for Bournemouth, follow the A338 into town. Turn L at roundabout past the station onto A35 Christchurch Rd, then Spa Rd or Sea Rd to the pier.

A bit more of a mellow option than it's neighbour, this is a potentially excellent, though fickle L&R beach break setup, with unpredictable banks structured by the pier. The L side can be pretty wedgy. Needs a good ground-swell but also works on east channel swell. There is a common cross-wind / rip combination. Easy access. Site of proposed, expensive artificial reef, subject to council approval in 2004.

SWANAGE BAY

Follow the same directions as for Kimmeridge from Bournemouth. Take the A351 to Swanage. Park up along the prom.

On very big SSW swells, there's a mainly R beach break on sand & rock. Rare channel east wind swells get in here too. Probably a better bet to head for Bournemouth. All standards.

BOURNEMOUTH

Head to the Pier, park up the hill.

Centre of S Coast surfing, the L side of the pier at high tide is the most consistent spot - a sometimes peaky L&R beach break. Picks up most swell & gets rippy and challenging if you catch it big. Best in autumn/winter. Crowds on weekends. Also works well in east storm swells.

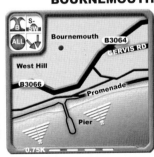

CHAPMAN'S: Head towards Kimmeridge then east on the A351 past the castle, L on B3069 to Worth Matravers. Hike.
Nice right-hander, and a fickle L reef. SW ground-swell helps it to get going. There are other options in this area, but accessibility is an issue. Big paddle-outs and dangerous currents. Advanced.

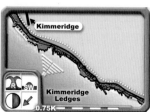

THE LEDGES: E from the Bay at Kimmeridge.
L&R reef break on rocky bottom, perfect for longboarders, breaking a long way out. Ls tend to be a lot better - can be hollow and barrelling. NB the rip that drags you right. Paddling is a mission when conditions are big. Friendly vibe for those who respect others.

KIMMERIDGE BAY: W on A35 from Bournemouth. L on A351 thro' Wareham & follow signs to Kimmeridge and the Bay.
Rock L&R breaking quite a way out, exposed to the big gales. Good long 1-200m rides if the other breaks are huge, otherwise pretty crowded as it's a well-known spot. Advanced, as rocks and difficult entry.

E9

just add water

boards, wetsuits, accessories & clothing

surf lessons, rental & repairs workshop

www.justaddwatersports.co.uk

stores:
norwich . plymouth . bournemouth . bath . reading
southampton . poole . guildford . brighton. swindon

THE BENCH

W on A35 from Bournemouth. L on A351 thro' Wareham & follow signs to Kimmeridge and the Bay. Walk round bottom of cliffs W out to the head.

Most days it's off limits from 9-5, due to army firing range. R reef breaking (short steep L too). Hollow, fast & gnarly break at best (which is admittedly rare) - light N winds help. Steep drops and barrels possible, as is dry-suck.

E9

WEYMOUTH

From Poole take the A351, then A352, then A353 round the bay to Weymouth. Park at the beach.

Beach break, best at low tide, with a big wrapping SW swell. Its offshore when everywhere else is blown out but needs huge swell. All levels. East channel wind-swell gets in well but a power south is good news here, if it's big.

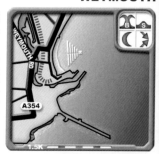

Secret south coast gem / Jim Michell / barefootmedia.co.uk

St Peter
Port
GUERNSEY

JERSEY
St He

GREVE DE LECQ

From St Helier go west on Victoria Ave to Beaumont. Go right at the roundabout on La Grande Route de St Pierre through St Peter & St Ouens to the bay.

When St Ouen's is closed out and the biggest SW winter storm swells are on, a grinding, fast, barreling R and a sucky, fast, short L get going here. Low tide & S wind a must. Watch out for the rocks and rips. Good surfers / loony grom bodyboarder break.

E10

PLEMONT

From St Helier take the same route to St Ouen. Go through the village, & take the Les Landes road. Turn R at signs for the bay.

In exactly the same conditions as Greve, although offshores are SE, this little cove turns on a R hand point reef wave of serious power and quality, breaking on shallow rock bottom. Steep takeoff, that you want to make sure you get right, quick bottom turn and then into a fast, long, barrelling section that then shoulders out. Watch out for your fins on the rocks. Advanced surfers only.

STINKY BAY

From St Helier take the same route to St Ouen. Turn L on B64 down the hill through L'Etacq & park by the slipway near the pub.

L hand point reef break, breaking off the rocks at the far N end of St Ouen's. Needs a solid winter NW swell & an offshore S/SE. Fairly tight takeoff, just off the rocks. Plus it's mega shallow at spring low tide (when it's at its most sucky). Up to mid is OK though. At best, will wall up nicely for a good, longish run. Be sure that if it's going off, the place will be packed. Intermediate surfers plus. Rocks at takeoff.

GOLDSMITHS

From St Helier take the same route to St Ouen. Turn L on B64 down the hill to L'Etacq. Fork L on B35 to the slipway car park.

Catch Goldies at high tide, on the top of the biggest spring tide, just R of the slip when the rest of St Ouen's is shoulder high, expect short, barrelling, hollow mainly R sandbar breaks. There are a couple of other named banks up here to look for too. Again, when it's on, you can guarantee a local-dominated crowd, although it should be fairly mellow if you follow the rules.

SECRETS

From St Helier take the A2/A12 to St Peters. Turn L on B41, Le Mont du Jubilee, to St Ouen's. Go R on B35 & park at La Grosse Tour.

On its day, with an incoming low spring tide and straight E offshores, a stunning Hossegor-style, barrelling R fires (breaks L&R but the R is the money break). The bigger the winter W/NW swell, the bigger it gets - holding well overhead. Sand-covered rock bottom holds the banks together consistently well. Competitive at the peak when it's on. Got to be good when it's big (if nothing else, to compete with the wired-in locals).

E10

WATERSPLASH

From St Helier take the A2/A12 to St Peters. Turn L on B41, Le Mont du Jubilee, to St Ouen's. Park up at the Splash.

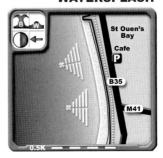

The centre of Jersey surfing. Very consistent beachbreak, with 2 main peaks going L&R. Works on all tides, more hollow 2 hours either side of low and fat at high. With any good W swell, you'll catch groomed lines coming in & overhead, whackable walls of perfection. Bit of a hike at low, but one cool spot. Great little cafe to watch the sunset from, or the crazy local groms catching the rebound wave off the wall.

LA ROCCO REEF

From St Helier take the A2/A12 to St Peters. Turn L on B41, Le Mont du Jubilee, to St Ouen's. Turn L & park at Le Braye slipway.

Out past La Rocco Tower, a rare big wave R breaks on a reef in huge winter storm swells, from mid to high tide. Awesome site if you're lucky enough to witness it - 15ft plus wall of pitted-faced gnarly wave - only ridden by a handful of locals. If you're a visitor,

you're unlikely to see this monster, but it's worth reminding the world that UK is home to some genuine big waves. Be sensible & surf the R beachbreaks at **Le Braye** instead!

PETIT PORT

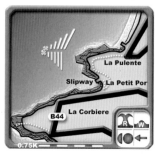

From St Helier take the A2 to St Aubin. Turn R on A13 through St Brelade, then B44 to Petit Port & park up at the slipway.

Paddle straight out from the slip to the peak (a rocky reef break - you won't miss it!). You have to catch the tide just right - a 28ft plus neap tide may just do it. In big autumn groundswells at mid-high, the R is steep, hollow, bowling and thick-lipped,

while the L is longer but less steep. Can be surfed up to 15ft, but it's challenging and expert only. Heavy currents.

CORBIERE POINT

Follow the same route from St Helier to Petit Port. Continue on to Corbiere, park up and hike down the rocks to the break.

Another big wave spot, accessed from Petit Port slipway. Needs a huge winter swell and best to hit it at high tides. If it's working, firstly, you'll see it (all 12-15ft of it!) and secondly, if you are expert, chuck your lid on, get your gun out, take a friendly (psycho) local, and go and ride the fast bowly rights or slower longer lefts. Fast moving currents. Hellmen only.

ST BRELADES BAY

From St Helier take the A2 to St Aubin. Turn R on A13 to St Brelade. Turn L on B45 and follow the road down to the bay carparks.

Beautiful scenic bay facing due South, home to small beachbreaks working in the big storm swells, when the wind is N, or more commonly, NW. Near the pier at the west end there's a nice, hollow little reef peak just after low tide. Also a nice peak near the headland in the middle. Surfing is banned in summer, as it is so busy with tourists.

143

L'ANCRESSE BAY & FORT LE MARCHANT

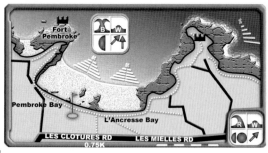

From St Peter Port, go R past the QE2 Marina on St Geroge's Esplanade & Les Banques. Turn L on Vale Road then take the right fork up Route Militaire to L'Ancresse Road. Follow signs to the bay carparks. For Fort le Marchant, drive to the head and park at the carpark on the E side to R of the Fort, overlooking the break.

The Fort needs a heavy winter storm swell - ideally a wrapping NE to pump in around the headland. When it's on (which is not very often), a hollow, sucky L hand point breaking well overhead on shallow rocky boulder bottom, therefore mid tide spot, but will work at high. Once you've taken the (at best, near vertical) drop, expect fast steep walls that then shoulder out in the deeper water. One of the few Channel Island breaks offshore in prevailing SW winds - this place would be super-consistent if only it worked with the groundswells. There's a rip that takes you straight to the peak but there's plenty of water moving out there so keep an eye out for the currents. Experienced surfers spot.

L'Ancresse Bay (and **Pembroke Bay** just past the rocky outcrop in the centre of the bay) can turn on nice little beachbreaks, mainly Rs, best on a dropping mid-high tide. There will probably be something in any N swell with even onshore SW winds but don't take that as a promise! L'Ancresse is more consistent and normally 1-2ft bigger than Pembroke. Good learner spot with few hazards.

From St Peter Port, go up Grange Road / De Beauvoir towards Castel. Go past the School and Folk Museum on your right on Route de Cobo. At the Coast Road turn R & follow the road round to the bay.

Well-known and often crowded surf spot. Experienced surfers, check out **The Knife,** the R point off the rocky boulders at the N end at high tide, - exposed to most Northerly swells, although maxes out at head-high. It's a short, makeable barrel that then shoulders out in the deep water, making it a great place for improvers wanting to move up to point-breaks. Hassles include the rocks (only surf at high tide, dudes) and the big crowds.

Head to the centre of the bay, in front of the carpark, for the most consistent beachbreak in Guernsey - best on a dropping mid tide on spring NW swells. Normally a couple of foot bigger than any of the other spots. Very crowded with all standards of surfers, but a blast after work on a warm summers' evening or a Sunday dawnie. Some rocks present a few problems but all in all, a straight-forward, laid-back 3-4ft beachbreak (doesn't hold much more than that before maxing out). Enjoy!

From St Peter Port, go up Grange Road / De Beauvoir towards Castel. Go past the School and Folk Museum on your right on Route de Cobo. At the Coast Road turn L on Rue D'Albecq into Vazon Road and park at the bay.

This is where it all happens - Vazon is Guernsey's swell magnet, with a number of different options for different standards:

Centres Reef, out from the Richmond kiosk, has a fickle reform wave in bigger swells - the outside R being a rare, bowling barrel, then it reforms on an inner sandbar for short L&Rs - the Rs being a better bet.

Vazon Reef, at the S end of the carpark, has a L&R, separated by the prominent Nipple Rock, slap-bang in the middle of the reef. Protected from adverse winds, both are high tide only breaks - best on springs, owing to the shallowness of the rocky reef, and both prefer a solid, straight NW swell. The R is generally more hollow and longer, the L has a steep drop, but shoulders out quickly.

However, in big, continuous swells, when the reef is maxing, follow the L to the south side of the reef for **T'Otherside** - a mellow R hand sandbar break, good for longboarders, that on it's day, can dish out long, glassy, walling 4ft perfection.

Something for everyone here, but be warned, when it's pumping, everyone will be there!

146

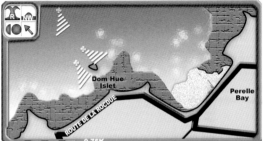

From St Peter Port, go up Grange Road / De Beauvoir towards Castel. Go past the School and Folk Museum on your right on Route de Cobo. At the Coast Road turn L on Rue D'Albecq through Vazon Bay and Perelle is the next bay round.

Guernsey's big wave spot with a series of reefs breaking approximately 3-400m offshore near the little islet of La Capelle (known as **Dom Hue**) - definitely for expert surfers only

Perelle Left & Right break either side of a rocky outcrop on a shallow rocky reef when there's a steady NW/N swell coming in. The R gets going earlier than the L, which is a steep-dropped, hollow barrel of a wave, packing quite a punch. Affected by the winds - needs light offshores to hold the lip up (especially the R). Bring your gun as it can be double overhead - it's always bigger when you get out there, and heavy currents run N to S...

Talking of guns, next break on the agenda is **Dom Hue,** and guess what, it's big! Out past Perelle, a rare, wind-affected big R breaks on a rocky reef in big storm & groundswells. Again, high tide avoids the rocks. It's a heart-stopping drop into a short, intense bowling R & then a thank you to the ocean gods! Very heavy currents, a shifting peak, 10ft white water on the inside - you name it. Hellmen only.

147

WALES

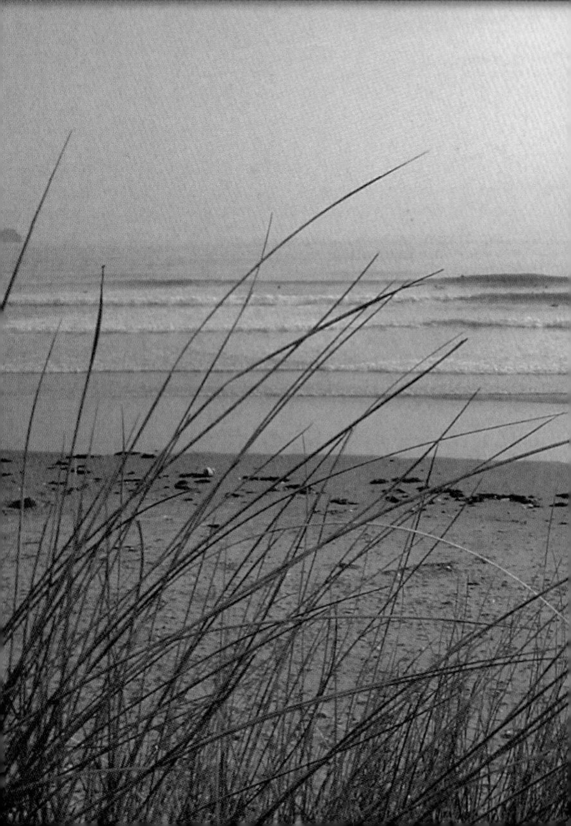

West Wales / The Gill

WALES

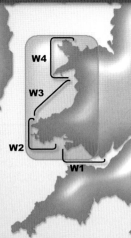

SURF DATA

Background

Wales has had a vibrant surf scene since the beginning, and the centre of this is The Gower in the southwest. No surprise that this peninsula and the Pembrokehsire coast offer the most consistent waves. As you head further north, wave possibilities decrease dramatically thanks to the intervention of Ireland. Ocean storms need to track as far south as possible for swell to hit with force.

When to go

Summer: Meagre offerings although southwest wind chop is common. **Autumn**: Solid west-norwest swells start to occur from October onwards and this is the best time to be a Welshman. It takes a pretty large system to get most spots firing but when its on, the whole southwest will come to life. Secret reefs will start to show, as will quality corner spots. **Spring**: Swell pattern becomes more spread out, and the water is at its coldest, but some great spring sessions are to be had. With the exception of Easter, uncrowded days are common. See our forecast page and make use of it before planning a trip. **Hazards -** Fickle surf, some pollution but much improved (check www.sas.org.uk).

M	Swell Range		Wind Pattern		Air		Sea	Crowd
	Feet	Dir'	Am	Pm	Lo	Hi		
J	2-6	wnw	variable	sw	-2	10	8-9	low
F	2-6	wnw	variable	sw	-2	10	8-9	low
M	2-6	wnw	variable	sw	3	13	10	low
A	0-4	wnw	variable	sw	6	16	11	med
M	0-4	wnw	variable	sw	9	17	13	med
J	0-3	nw-sw	variable	sw	13	23	14	hi
J	0-3	nw-sw	variable	sw	15	25	16	hi
A	0-3	nw-sw	variable	sw	15	25	16	hi
S	1-6	wnw-w	variable	sw	13	24	15	med
O	2-8	wnw	variable	sw	12	18	15	med
N	2-8	wnw	variable	sw	8	14	13	low
D	2-8	wnw	variable	sw	4	12	10	low

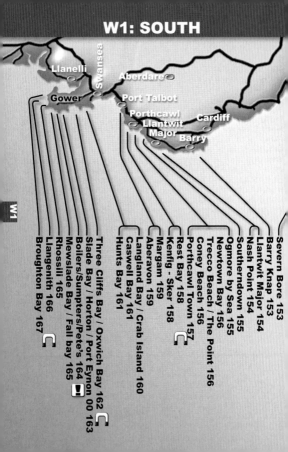

W1: SOUTH

Swansea

Llanelli

Gower

Aberdare

Port Talbot

Porthcawl

Llantwit Major

Cardiff

Barry

W1

THE SEVERN BORE

On the Welsh side, from Chepstow the A48 follows the path of the river, head for Blakeny and get in wherever looks good!

V big spring tides can send a bit of a mythical wave up the River Severn starting 15kms S of Gloucester at Awre with rides of 3 miles plus quite possible! The aim of the game is to stay on as long as possible. There's even a Bore Riders Club.

W1

BARRY KNAP

From M4 Jct 33 take A4232, then A4050 following signs for Barry then the Knap. Plenty of parking above the pebbles.

Sucky, but inconsistent shore-break with heavy close-outs, breaking on sand & pebble bottom. Gets waves on very big SW swells or storm swells brought in by strong winds in the Bristol Channel. All standards.

Jim Brooks Surfboards and Repairs - Cardiff - 07970 420998

LLANTWIT MAJOR

From M4 Jct 33 take A4232 at first junction take A48, follow signs for Llantwit Major and then the beach. On a reasonable sized swell, awesome R breaks off the rocks to the left of the beach over sand and reef bottom at low tide. As the tide climbs there are various L&R peaks. Does get busy. Watch out for the rocks at mid to high tide, and some localism. Intermediate plus break.

City Surf, Castle Arcade, Cardiff - 02920 342068
Jim Brooks Surfboards and Repairs - Cardiff (Via City Surf)
Phone 07970 420998

NASH POINT

From M4 Jct 33 take A4232 then A48 & follow signs for Llantwit Major. Go R on B4265 then L to Marcross. Go past the church to the car park.

A very rocky spot that can produce a challenging, intense R at low tide, breaking on rock bottom. Hollow ride into shallow water. Gets overhead here. V inconsistent with small takeoff point and an advanced wave so not too crowded.

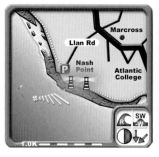

SOUTHERNDOWN

M4 Jct 35, take the A473 then B4524 to Ogmore-by-Sea & on to Southerndown, carpark by the beach.

Various shifting peaks, best on the climbing tide with a strong swell, but is a bit of a swell magnet. The break L of the rivermouth in front of the carpark can be a peeling, hollow L over reef/rock. Beware rocks at high tide. Strong currents too. Something for everyone.

Turtle Reef (.co.uk), Bells Road, Bridgend - 01656 655526

OGMORE-BY-SEA

M4 Jct 35, take the A473 then B4524 then follow signs to Ogmore-by-Sea carpark by the beach right on the rivermouth.

Various peaks on the main beach breaking on sand and/or reef bottom. On a strong clean swell there's a long left into the rivermouth and a good right. Ideal longboard wave. Normally uncrowded unless the river mouth is working (advanced surfers). Strong currents. All standards.

NEWTON BAY & TRECCO BEACH

Turn off the M4 at Jct 37 onto A4229 to Porthcawl. Take signs to Newton. Limited parking at beach.

Various peaks in both these bays on either side of Newton Point. Handles a strong W wind for swell. Rarely crowded. Watch out for the rip dragging you away from the point & pollution. **Trecco Beach** has various peaks at mid tide. Needs reasonable swell. A bit rippy. All levels.

Xtreme clothing & equipment
www.tantrum.co.uk
Made for breaking stuff!

THE POINT AND CONEY BEACH

Turn off the M4 at Jct 37 onto A4229 to Porthcawl. Follow A4106 all the way to the harbour.

Hollow R breaks on sandy reef bottom. Fast take-off that wraps off the rocks from mid to high. Too much wind is messy and the wave sections. Can get busy, only holds a small number, some localism. Expert break. Water cleanliness issue. **Coney Beach**, tucked in behind the harbour wall, is the

only place to go to get shelter from the howling SW winds so it gets crowded. Works for a few hours from mid tide on the climb.

156

PORTHCAWL TOWN

Off the Esplanade in town, north from the harbour wall before Rest Bay.

A sucky and very short wave can occasionally be found at high tide just in front of the esplananade. Good for bodyboarding.

All levels, but dumpy.

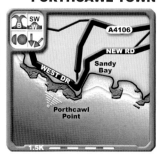

Simon Tucker Surf Academy, School & Hire - 07815 289761
Jim Brooks Surfboards and Repairs - Cardiff - 07970 420998

Crab Island / The Gill

REST BAY

From M4 Jct 37, follow signs for Porthcawl town then Rest Bay, car park overlooking beach.

Various good L&R peaks on sand bottom, but badly affected by W winds. Picks up the most swell in this area & v consistent so v crowded, especially in front of the slipway. Some localism. Strong rips on the rocks at high tide leave a small bay in front of slipway. Beginners plus.

Porthcawl Marine, New Road, Porthcawl - 01656 728392
Double Overhead, Surf & Skate, New Road - 01656 782220
Rush - Kite & Surf, rushextreme.co.uk - 01656 773311

KENFIG - SKER

From M4 Jct 37 follow signs for Porthcawl town. Just after roundabout with Texaco garage turn R for Kenfig golf course. Follow lane, turn R at end & cross into carpark. Walk across dunes.

Similar to Rest - L&R beachies on sandy bottom, but with a smaller beach area. Much less crowded (mainly due to the 20 min walk over the dunes). Watch out for the rocks at high tide. Intermediate break.

Turtle Reef (.co.uk), Bells Road, Bridgend - 01656 655526

MARGAM

M4 Jct 38, follow signs for the Cemetery and Margam, park at the train track and walk through industrial site. Risky parking.

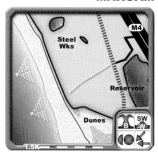

Picks up a similar amount of swell to Rest Bay. Ls & Rs break close to the shore on sandy bottom, holding up to 6ft waves. Rarely crowded as limited parking and a big 20 min walk through the industrial estate. Nice! Best on incoming tide. Sensitive to wind. Intermediate plus.

ABERAVON BEACH / HARBOUR WALL

M4 Jct 40, follow signs for Aberavon & the beach. Lots of parking along the prom. Park at the harbour for The Wall.

Miles of sandy beach. Surfable on most tides, and can get good on the breakwater at high. **The Wall** is a consistent, fast, wedgy L that joins a hollow closeout section on to the beach on sand & rock bottom. Works well at mid (sometimes at high water on small tides). Crowds & tight local crew. Intermediate plus.

LANGLAND BAY & CRAB ISLAND

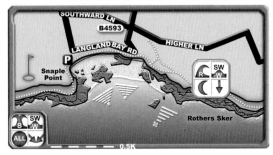

At M4 Jct 42 take A483 to Swansea. Head along the waterfront on A4067 (signs for Mumbles), then take the A4593 to Langland Bay Rd and follow it to the beach.

Langland Bay is one of the busiest spots in Wales. Needs a medium to big swell. Shore break at high tide, reef at mid tide and mid-low the centre of the bay is working. Strong rip out to sea in centre of bay. Fickle in summer. Heavy crowds & some localism. Limited parking. Intermediate surfers.

A fabled, high-quality R can appear off **Crab Island** at low tide breaking on rocky reef bottom in reasonable swells - watch the shallow rocks. Handles some size too (6ft plus). Even tighter takeoff & v localized. Occasional pollution issue. Advanced surfers only.

Crab Island Surfboards - Since 1977
crabislansurfboards.com - 01792204627

JP Surfboards - jpsurfboards.co.uk - 07813195217

Langland Cove Guest House, Rotherslade Road - 01792366003

City Surf, Picton Arcade, Swansea - 01792654169

CASWELL BAY

Take same directions as for Langland. Go past the Langland Bay Rd turn-off on B4593 to Caswell Bay. Small car park opposite beach.

L&R sandy bottom beach breaks - R side is often a good bet. Needs a medium to big W or SW swell to get going. Pretty fickle though. Holds a small crowd, but a relaxed vibe. Gets rocky at low, although little surf anyway. Good beginners spot.

Hot Dog Surf Shop, Pennard Rd, Kittle - 01792 234073

W1

HUNTS BAY

M4 Jct 42, through Swansea, follow signs for South Gower via Killay (A4118) to Oxwich. Turn off via Pennard to Southgate.

Nice little L&R reef break, needs a medium swell & only works mid-high tide. Even then, watch out as it is pretty shallow & rocky. Doesn't hold big crowds, but being very inconsistent, is rarely crowded anyway. Intermediate/ advanced break.

THREE CLIFFS BAY

M4 Jct 42, through Swansea, follow signs for South Gower via Killay (A4118). On Sth Gower Rd towards Oxwich, park at Penmaen & follow signs to beach.

Secluded bay, home to good L&R rivermouth sandbar break. Only really works on a big or stormy swell. Beware v dangerous current outwards by the stream - people have been lost. Limited & unsecure parking plus 15 min walk in. Intermediate/advanced..

OXWICH BAY

M4 Jct 42, through Swansea, follow signs for South Gower via Killay (A4118). Sth Gower Rd then signposted Oxwich Rd. Paid parking in season.

V large SW winter storm swells produce various A-frame options. Hollow wave at high tide. Handles strong W winds & good shelter from the headland. Big crowd, (often 100 surfers in the water if good!). All standards should get a wave here.

Shockwaves Surfboards - Wynn Morris, Near Oxwich - 01792371345

PORT EYNON, HORTON & SLADE BAY

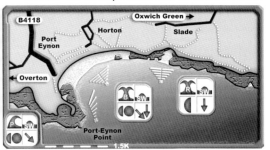

M4 Jct 42, through Swansea, follow signs for South Gower via Killay (A4118). Sth Gower Rd follow signs for Port Eynon, Turn off for Horton, car park at the beach, or get to Slade via Oxwich.

The Bay needs a lot of swell with easy shallow rides. Predominantly sandbar beach-breaks. All standards.

The Point is a good R point break off the headland on rocky sand bottom. Steep drop and quick first section, then shoulders out.

Horton Beach has, on a very big swell, a hollow shore break wave on sandy bottom. Quite a pile-driver on occasions. Pretty spot.

Slade Beach also needs a big swell for its L&R peaky A-frames to work, only access along coast path from Horton or via Slade. Rocky.

North Gower / The Gill

BOILERS

M4 Jct 42, through Swansea, follow signs for South Gower via Killay (A4118) into Port Eynon. R into Overton then a cliff walk.

Serious left on shallow reef bottom. Difficult access, risky take off in shallow water but breaks into deeper water. Small numbers only, mainly local. Strong rip away from the peak, beware of climbing tide against the rocks, park respectfully. Advanced surfers only. You are also in the area for **Pete's**: a quality reef that you can have the joy of finding yourself!

SUMPTERS REEF

M4 Jct 42, through Swansea, follow signs for South Gower via Killay (A4118) into Port Eynon. R into Overton then a cliff walk.

Mirror image of Boilers - a R hander on reef bottom. Difficult access, slightly deeper water and easier going than other reefs. The lip packs a surprising punch! Small numbers only & mainly local. Park respectfully. Advanced surfers only. This stretch of the Gower contains some of the finest reefs in Wales, so we haven't been too specific about how to find them. If you get here please show respect to all.

MEWSLADE - FALL BAY

Take A4118 Sth Gower Rd. Just before Port Eynon, take B4247 to Rossili. Park up & head L through the fields, 20 min walk.

On a big swell with some S in it, this small bay can produce small but good, peaky A-frames, sheltered from northerlies. Never crowded due to the lack of consistency & the long walk in - it's a beautiful spot too. Intermediate surfers.

RHOSSILI BAY

Take A4118 Sth Gower Rd. Just before Port Eynon, take B4247 to Rossili. Park on headland & walk down the cliff path.

Peaky A-frame L&R's on sand, generally a little smaller & weaker than Llangennith, but there are plenty of options and it handles the crowds. Sheltered on light southerly winds. Prefers huge SW swells. All levels.

ALDER

DESIGNED FOR DREAMS

LLANGENNITH & THREE PEAKS

M4 Jct 47 to Gorseinon then Gowerton, follow the North Gower road to Llangennith beach. Park at Hillend caravan park, access through the dunes.

Llangennith is generally the indicator spot for the Gower, picking up the most swell in this area. A huge beach that is very popular with all surfers, plenty of A-frame peaks to go round in most conditions. Very consistent waves as well as numbers of surfers/ water users, especially in summer. A few strong rips to be aware of too.

At the far north end of Llangennith, **Three Peaks** provide solid lefts and rights close together, breaking on sandbars. Each peak only holds small numbers, so soon gets busy, even with the 20min dune walk. A bit more challenging so intermediate plus peaks. Rocking surf spot with much heritage & charm.

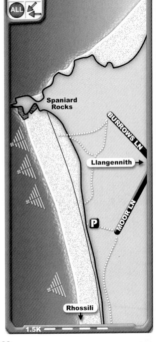

PJ's, pjsurfshop.co.uk,
open all year - 01792386669
Surfline™ - 09016031603 - calls 60p/min at all times
Hydro Active Surfboards - Chris Beynon, via Hot Dog, Kittle
Call- 01792234073

BROUGHTON BAY

M4 Jct 47, take the A4240 then B4296 to Gowerton. Follow Nth Gower Road through Llangennith village & follow signs for Broughton. Park at caravan site.

Mainly L long, peeling wave below the headland, breaking on sand/reef bottom (can be 2-300m rides). Cranks on S storm swells (does handle some W in the swell). Strong rip away from main peak. Longboard central. Crowds if Llangennith is maxed. Intermediate.

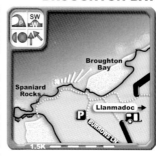

Gower Overview / The Gill

Cardigan

Goodwich
Fishguard

St Davids

Carr

St Brides
Milford Haven
Pembroke
Tenby

ABEREIDDY

From Haverfordwest, take the A487 (or from Fishguard) until you see signposts at Croesgoch to Portheiddy. Follow the beach road & park up.

Great spot on a wrapping SW swell but can just handle a rare N too. Sheltered from S winds. There's a pretty hollow, sucky L here, breaking on sand-covered reef. Gets overhead. Rarely busy, handles small crowds. Intermediate to advanced break.

WHITESAND BAY

From Haverfordwest, A487 to St Davids, then B4583 to the beach car park.
V popular spot that produces plenty of waves with a relaxed crowd. Consistent L&R A-frames over sandbars. Big W swells get it cranking. Often crowded, especially with tourists in summer. All levels.
Ma Sime's Surf Hut, High Street, St Davids - masurf.co.uk - 01437 720433
Simon Noble Surfboards (SNS), St Davids - www.snsboards.co.uk 07866 737935
SNS Surf Shop & Camping, St Davids - 07866 737935

169

PENYCWM & NEWGALE SANDS

From Haverfordwest, take A487 all the way to Penycwm.

There are many peaks up and down **Newgale Sands** with several car parks and good facilities. A bit of a swell magnet, therefore very consistent. Best on the dropping tide. Mild currents. On the pebbles at high tide, but can be surfable at the south end. Copes well with its fairly relaxed crowd. Something for all standards here.

Penycwm has a sucky, hollow right that works for a few hours on the climbing tide at the north end of Newgale Sands, below the cliffs. Beware of fast climbing tide on the rocks. Mainly locals, only holds a small crowd. Intermediate / Advanced. Other options in this area for the intrepid. Get out there!

W2

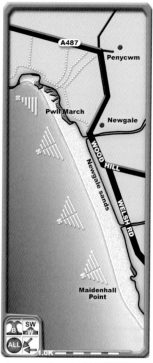

Newsurf Surf & Hire, Newgale, newsurf.co.uk - 01437721398

DRUIDSTON

M4 Jct 49, take the A48/A40 to Haverfordwest. Take A487 then turn off at Simpsons Cross to Druidston.

When Newgale is blown out, this spot can offer a little shelter, yet with more power than Broadhaven. It's a fickle spot however, and is best in bigger W/SW swells at low-mid tide. Beware of the rocks at high tide, and mild currents. Middle of nowhere, intermediate plus spot.

Seaweed Surf Shop, Quay Street, Haverfordwest - 01437760774

BROAD HAVEN

M4 Jct 49, take the A48/A40 to Haverfordwest. B4341 to Broad Haven. Car park at Enfield Rd.
When everywhere is maxed, or on a very solid swell, manageable and hollow rides can sometimes be found. Best on dropping tide. Tends to close out at low tide. Popular with beginners, copes with a small crowd. Be aware of other water users. Improvers.
Havensports, Marine Rd, havensports.co.uk 01437781354

Anchor Guest House, Seafront, anchorguesthouse.co.uk - 01437 781476
Jim Brooks Surfboards and Repairs, Via Havensports - 07970 420998

MARLOES SANDS

M4 Jct 49, take the A48/A40 to Haverfordwest. B4327 just before Dale, take the signs to Marloes & the car park. 10min walk.

A good spot with various peaks, good on most stages of the climbing tide except extreme high. Beware of high tide on the rocks, can cover whole bay. Rarely surfed, small crowd of locals. Take a trip N to **St Brides Bay** for busy fun peaks.

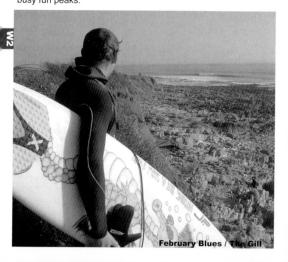

February Blues / The Gill

WESTDALE BAY

M4 Jct 49, take the A48/A40 to Haverfordwest. Take B4327 to Dale. Park in town then walk to the bay & down the cliff.

A secluded bay that offers a little shelter from southerly winds. Hollow rights and lefts off the rocks on a climbing tide. Only holds a small crowd, can get busy when good. Dangerous currents and heavy shore dump at high tide. Intermediate / advanced.

Game On, Riverside Market, Haverfordwest - 01437 779 020

FRESHWATER WEST

M4 Jct 49, take the A48, then A40 to St Clears. A477 to Pembroke, then B4320 to the beach car park.

Picks up the most swell in Pembrokeshire with several sandbar peaks on the main beach and reefs. V consistent therefore gets V busy. Strong rips, various peaks on the rocks (check the S end). Just off a big army firing range! Intermediate / advanced.

Waves 'N' Wheels, Main Street, Pembroke - 01646622066
Game On, Riverside Market, Haverfordwest - 01437779020
Outer Reef Surf School, outerreefsurfschool.com
01646680070 / 07769903653

BROADHAVEN SOUTH

A477 from St Clears all the way to Pembroke, then B4319 and follow signs. Park above Broad Haven beach.

Various L&R sandbar peaks on a solid SW swell. Sometimes produces a sucky left reef break off the rocks but it's a fickle spot. Likes a light W /NW wind. A long way to go if it's flat (not uncommon)! Even so, attracts the crowds. Intermediate surfers plus.

FRESHWATER EAST

M4 Jct 49, take the A48, then A40 to St Clears. A477 to Pembroke, then B4584 into the village. Park at the dunes.

Only really works in the winter on big or westerly storm swells, producing a barrelling L&R on shifting sandbars. Rarely crowded, due to the fact that it's often flat! Water quality can be an issue, particularly after storms. Beginner / intermediate spot.

174

MANORBIER

M4 Jct 49, take the A48, then A40 to St Clears. A477/478 thro' Tenby, then follow A4139 to Manorbier. Park at the bay.

Various consistent, fun peaks with a good R off the rocks, breaking on rocky reef bottom. Can be mellow, as is popular with longboarders. Often busy, especially when working in the summer. Beginner peaks, the R is intermediate.

Underground Surf Shop, Waterloo House, Brewery Terrace, Saundersfoot - 01834814484

TENBY SOUTH BEACH

M4 Jct 49, take the A48, then A40 to St Clears. A477/478 to Tenby & park at the beach.

Gets good on the rare occasional W or SW storm swell, offering a little shelter when everywhere is blown out. Nice, peaky, shoulder-high L&Rs on sand bottom which can barrel. Not too crowded but busy in the summer with tourists. Beginners upwards.

Underground Surf Shop, Church St, Tenby - 01834844234

W3: WEST

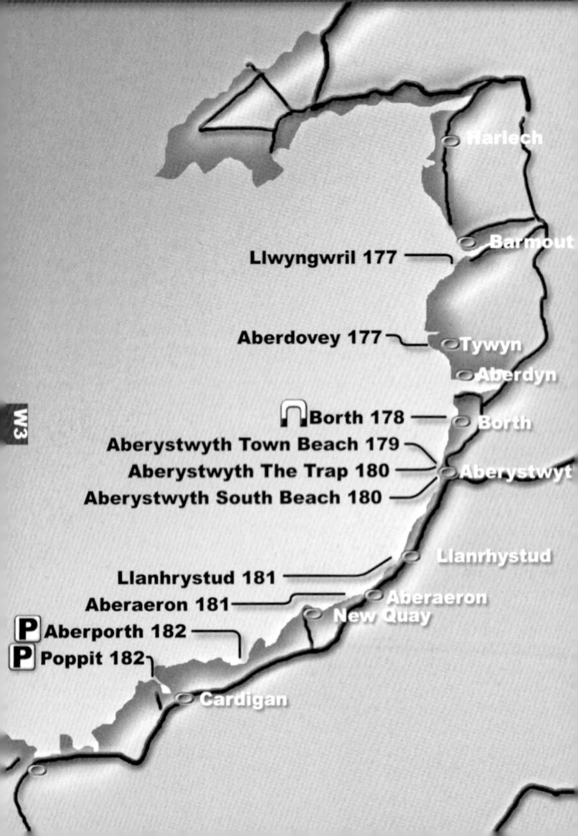
Harlech
Barmout
Llwyngwril 177
Aberdovey 177
Tywyn
Aberdyn
Borth 178
Borth
Aberystwyth Town Beach 179
Aberystwyth The Trap 180
Aberystwyt
Aberystwyth South Beach 180
Llanrhystud
Llanhrystud 181
Aberaeron 181
Aberaeron
New Quay
P Aberporth 182
P Poppit 182
Cardigan

LLWYNGWRIL

From M54 at Shrewsbury, take A5 then A458/A470 to Dolgellau. A493 S into Llwyngwril & head for the caravan site.

An awesome L grinds off the point over shallow reef bottom, when the swell is strong enough. Hollow fast and long barrels! Also a R breaks on the reef and links up into the shore break. Quality break with quality local surfers when it's firing. Advanced spot.

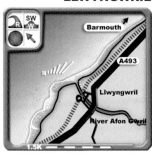

Stormriders, www.storm-riders.co.uk - 01970626363

ABERDOVEY / TYWYN

Head for Machynlleth and then take the A493 to Aberdovey. Follow the road up for access at Tywyn.

Huge stretch of beach with plenty of left and right beach-break peaks when there's a good swell running. Far left end offers better quality waves. 1-4ft, consistent. Only busy in the summer, copes with a crowd. Beginner / intermediate.

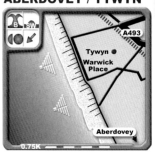

The Beach House - Surf & Kite, New St - 01654767030

BORTH BEACH

Take the same directions as for Aberystwyth. Head out of town on A487, then L on B4572 to Borth. Go N on High St to the beach.

A huge beach that produces mellow L&R beachies on shifting sandbars. A little fickle but nevertheless it can attract all west to southwest swells. Borth will work at most points of tide, although best power and shape is found on the push.

Great spot for learning with a laidback set-up and cool local crew that are well spread-out.

1-4ft. Quite consistent for this area, but still not that reliable. Beginners upwards. Handles any number of surfers with its many peaks.

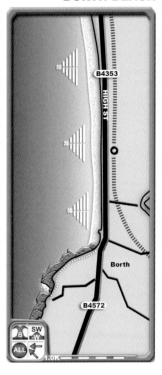

ABERYSTWYTH TOWN BEACH

From M5 Jct 6/7 take the A44 all the way! Get onto Marina Terrace for the beach.

To the north end of the beach is **Bath Rocks** - a fast right best at high tide. Nearby is **Queens**, a popular left. Both break on sand & reef bottom. 1-5ft. Fairly consistent. Can get busy. Intermediate plus.

Freedom Sport & Surf, Alexandra Rd, Aberystwyth - 01970612802
Stormriders, www.storm-riders.co.uk - 01970626363

West Wales / The Gill

ABERYSTWYTH SOUTH BEACH

Wherever you are heading from just follow signs for Aberystwyth (A44 most popular), then follow the relevant signs to the beach (near the Castle).

The Wall: Beside the sea wall below the Castle is a short fast Left on sand and rock, working from mid tide upwards.

Nearby **Castle Point** can also produce a right at times on sand and rock. 1-5ft. Inconsistent. Rarely too busy. Heavy shore-break at times.

Stormriders, www.storm-riders.co.uk - 01970 626363

THE TRAP

From M5 Jct 6/7 at Worcester, take the A44 all the way to Aberystwyth. Once in town, head for the castle on Marina Terrace, then S to the N harbour wall.

Most consistent break in the area, best on the dropping tide, can produce steep, hollow & barrelling L&Rs breaking on sand & rock bottom close to shore. Bodyboarder time at high tide when its a gromfest. Strong rip from the river. Intermediate plus level.

Stormriders, www.storm-riders.co.uk - 01970626363

LLANRHYSTUD

Take the A487 S from Aberystwyth or N from Cardigan. Park at the campsite in the village & walk N on the coast path.

Just to the right of the beach you will find a good left around the corner, breaking into deeper water on sand & rocky bottom. Fairly rocky, can have heavy shore-break at high tide. Rarely busy even in summer. Good, if fickle intermediate spot.

ABERAERON

Take the A487 S from Aberystwyth or N from Cardigan. Take Tabernacle St down to the front.

NW facing pebble beach that offers some shelter when other spots are maxed, best on the dropping tide. Really needs a big SW swell. Not hugely consistent. Beware of rocks at high tide. Got to be fairly intrepid to get there! Intermediate / Advanced.

ABERPORTH

From Cardigan take the A487 north, turn off and follow signs to Aberporth.

Low to mid tide beach-break needing a big swell and southerly winds. Particularly good on a super-strong southwesterly swell. Various peaks. 2-4ft. Inconsistent. Can get busy, especially in the summer. Beginner / Intermediate.

Wet Spot(.co.uk), Bryn Arfor, Aberporth - 01239811911

W3

POPPIT SANDS

Head towards Cardigan then follow signs for St Dogmaels along B4546 then on to Poppit Sands

Left and right beach-break peaks on any tide and a good west swell. Can be good after northwest gales, always best on a dropping tide. Rivermouth current can be used to get out the back. 2-5ft. Inconsistent. Copes well, Can get busy in the summer.

Strong visible rip currents, especially near river mouth. Beginner / Intermediate.

Cardigan Sports, High Street, Cardigan - 01239615996

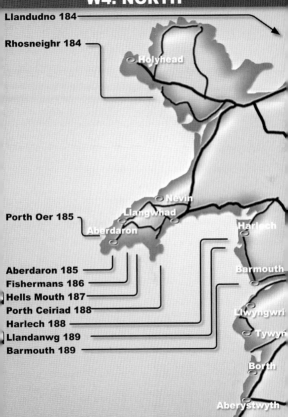

Llandudno 184

Rhosneighr 184

Holyhead

Nevin

Llangwnadl

Porth Oer 185

Aberdaron

Harlech

Aberdaron 185

Barmouth

Fishermans 186

Hells Mouth 187

Porth Ceriad 188

Llwyngwril

Harlech 188

Llandanwg 189

Tywyn

Barmouth 189

Borth

Aberystwyth

LLANDUDNO

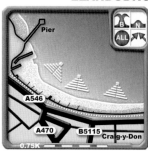

Wherever you're coming from head towards Colwyn Bay then follow signs to Llandudno.

Left and right beach-break setup on most tides. Both beaches are fairly sheltered and lacking waves, but the north beach can work for surfing on a big westerly storm swell. Right corner gets the most size. Uncrowded, 1-4t if on. Beginners plus.

Escape Surfwear, Mostyn St, Llandudno - 01492877149

RHOSNEIGHR

Take A5 from Wrexham, or A55 from Chester, to Bangor. Cross the bridge. Follow A5 then L on A4080 to Rhosneighr.

Broken up by rocks, this exposed SW-facing beach picks up a lot of swell. Various L&R peak options of varying quality & consistency. Badly affected by prevailing strong winds though. Rips are strong here. All standards. Could try back down the road for similar at **Aberffraw**.

Fun Sport, Rhosneighr - 01407810899

W4

WHISTLING SANDS, PORTH OER

As Aberdaron. From here head north east and follow the coast road to Methlem, between Anelog and Rhydllos.

Left and right beach-break peaks on middle tides. Needs a strong SW storm to get it going, good when hells mouth is maxed or blown out. 1-4ft. Inconsistent. All levels. Only holds a small crowd when working.

ABERDARON

Take the same directions as for Hells Mouth. Go through Pwllheli then turn R on B4413 & follow signs.

Produces similar waves to Hells Mouth - various L&R shifting sandbar and sand-covered reef peaks with a good R off the rocks. Pretty open beach which does have some heavy currents. Never too busy & all standards can get a wave here.

185

FISHERMANS

Take the same directions as for Aberdaron. In the village follow the rd round & back E to Llanfaelrhys & ask a local where to walk.

Good fast and hollow right hander breaks here off an unfriendly rocky spot. It is difficult to access cleanly and without losing skin as a result. Very often a wave here - the reef handles all swell and tides. Only holds a small crowd, often gets busy, some localism. Isolated spot so advanced surfers only.

West Wales / Pete Adams

HELLS MOUTH

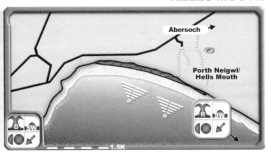

Take the A470 N from Dolgellau to Festiniog then get onto the A487 to the A497 and follow it to Pwllheli. Take the A499 to Abersoch & follow signs for the beach.

Main Beach is usually the busiest spot in North Wales. Vast sandy beach with plenty of peaky L&R beach-breaks & some reef action. Always crowded & rippy, and good on north to northeast winds.

The Reef in the south end of the beach off the map, is one of the most consistent spots around - good hollow R with crowded take-off point, on sand-covered rock bottom.

The Corner is a rocky takeoff L that finishes over sand. Handles big swell & often reaches as far as the reef. Its right at the south-east end of the beach.

West Coast Surf (.co.uk) School & Shop, Abersoch - 01758713067

Great Accommodation Tanrallt 01758 713527 www.tanrallt.com

On the Lleyn peninsula, take the A497 on to the A499 to Abersoch. From here head out to Cilan Uchaf, parking on the cliffs overlooking break.

Some good lefts, with various fast take offs and hollow rides off the cliffs.

High tide on a north wind best. It is a steep beach. Beach-break seclusion for solid southwest swells. 1-4ft. All levels. Fairly consistent.

HARLECH

As for Barmouth but stay on the A496 until Harlech, follow signs to the beach.

A big sandy beach with plenty of peaks, though doesn't pick up that much swell. It handles any number but rarely busy anyway as not a favoured spot.

1-4ft. Improvers. Inconsistent.

LLANDANWG

From M54 at Shrewsbury, take A5 then A458/A470 to Dolgellau. A496 through Barmouth up the coast. Good caravan site.

Sometimes great L&R sandbar/reef break at the rivermouth. Best on the dropping tide. Fickle due to shifting sand. Some shelter from southerlies though. Offshore is SE. Not too busy. S of the rivermouth for other options. Intermediate spot.

BARMOUTH

From M54 at Shrewsbury, take A5 then A458/A470 to Dolgellau. A496 into Barmouth. Car parking on Marine Pde.

A variety of sandbar L&R options, best on the dropping tide in the winter months (don't forget your rubber!). Mixed quality due to the shifting sands at this big exposed beach (especially near the rivermouth at S end) but it does attract swell. Beginner / intermediate.

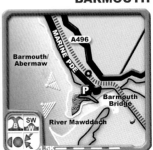

W4

SCOTLAND

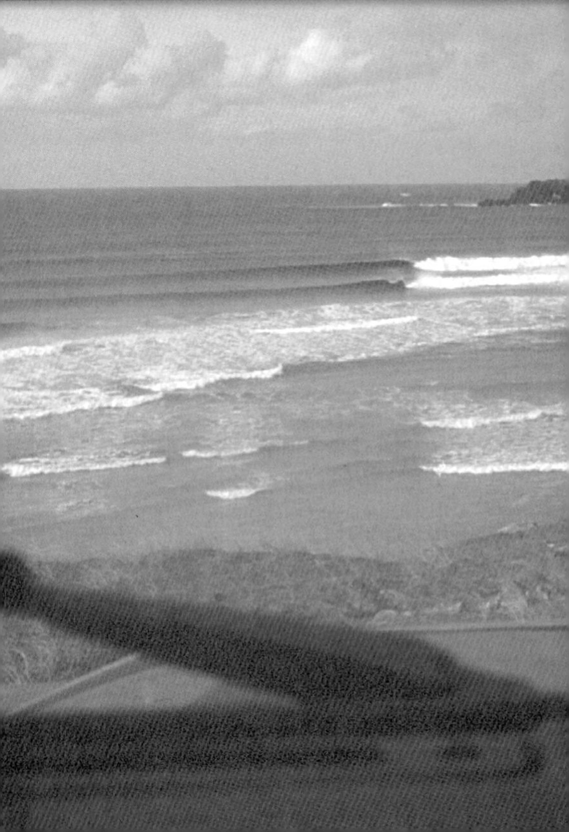

Isle of Lewis / Pete Adam

SCOTLAND

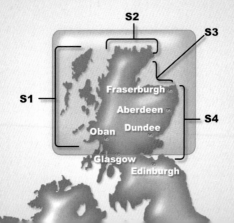

WEST COAST SURF DATA

Background

Scotland's west coast, without a doubt, hosts some of the biggest and best surf in Europe. It's contorted chain of islands and peninsula are at the end of one of the longest fetches in the Atlantic, and present every possible angle to the wind. This means if you cannot find a wave and off-shore conditions here, move continent. An ancient Celtic culture, bleakly beautiful scenery and extreme isolation make this one of Europe's last real surf adventures. To sum up: West Coast Scotland is awesome.

When to go

Summer: The Western Isles pick up any pulse going, so it is relatively consistent even at this time. **Autumn**: Huge long-period swells arrive constantly from October onwards, often accompanied by gale or storm force winds. Luckily corner spots can protect from the mostly southwest conditions but be prepared for severe adventure. **Winter**: A hard core version of autumn. **Spring**: Swell pattern becomes more spread out, and the water is at its coldest, but some great spring sessions are to be had.

Hazards

Extreme cold. Storm conditions. Isolation. Quality whiskey. Seals.

M	Swell Range		Wind Pattern		Air		Sea	Crowd
	Feet	Dir'	Am	Pm	Lo	Hi		
J	2-12	wnw	sw	sw	-2	8	6	low
F	2-12	wnw	sw	sw	-2	8	6	low
M	2-12	wnw	sw	sw	3	11	7	low
A	0-5	wnw	sw	sw	6	14	9	low
M	0-5	wnw	sw	sw	9	16	10	low
J	0-5	nw-sw	sw	sw	12	21	12	low
J	0-4	nw-sw	sw	sw	14	23	13	low
A	0-4	nw-sw	sw	sw	14	23	14	low
S	1-14	wnw-w	sw	sw	12	20	14	low
O	2-14	wnw	sw	sw	7	14	12	low
N	2-14	wnw	sw	sw	2	13	10	low
D	2-14	wnw	sw	sw	0	12	8	low

Outer Hebrides / Peter Adams

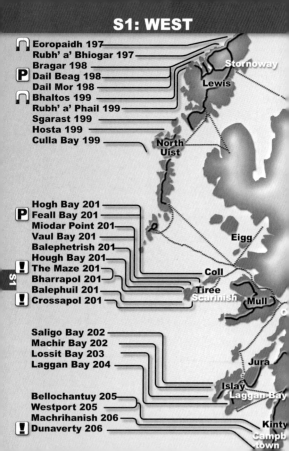

S1: WEST

S1

Stornoway
Lewis
North Uist
Eigg
Coll
Tiree
Scarinish
Mull
Jura
Islay
Laggan Bay
Kinty
Campb
town

EOROPAIDH

4 Hour ferry from Ullapool to Isle of Lewis: From Stornoway go N up the A857 to the top of the island.

The main spot on Lewis. Beautiful clear water beach-break peaks that line up and barrel if the wind is right (southeast to east is best). It can get serious and big, and there are reef breaks at either end. If it is flat here try another continent.

BARABHAS/RUHBA BHIOGAR

On Lewis: Head up the A857 from Stornoway to the end. The road splits at Barabhas but you keep on fighting through on the track round the Loch.

Mystic reef break off rocky outcrops, handling any swell size from the north to northwest. East to south winds are best, and higher tides. Advanced only. This spot gets big and hairy. Plenty of undocumented, awesome, consistent spots in the area. All you need is woolly clothing, a good suit, and a heavy duty vehicle.

197

BRAGAR

On Lewis: From Stornoway, up the A857 till it ends. Left to village.

More approachable beachbreak in the shadow of the cemetary. It's a beautiful spot with its palpable Celtic heritage. Consistent, and fun. Any tide. All levels. This is a good spot to head when the prevailing southwesterlies are blowing the life out of Eoropaidh and other beaches.

DAIL BEAG

On Lewis: Head W down the A858 from Bragar. Turn off right after about 8K. Carpark.

Secluded little bay with pebbly/rocky beach-break achieving hollow perfection in any southwest to north swell, with winds southwest through east. There are reefs in this area that can go off on their day. Consistent spot. 2-10ft. Advanced. A few minutes west is **Dail Mor**, worth a look in similar conditions, and offering beach-break and reef quality. Popular spot, and the water is beautiful.

On Lewis: Head due W from Stornoway on the A858 then the B8011 to the village of Miabhaig. Turn off N to Cliobh (**Cliff**).

Stunning beach-break ideal in southeast winds and north oriented swells at any tide. Its a deep bay protected from destructive winds. The wave can get hollow and carries some weight. Lefts and rights. 2-10ft. Consistent. Never busy, but one of the most popular spots on Lewis. All levels but for advanced only if big.

MANGURSTADH/RUHBA PHAIL

See directions for Cliff. Head from here to Mangurstadh then due N up the track to the end.

Hard-core spot handling any size you care to surf.

In a big southwest wind and if there is plenty of size, head down to **Sgarasta** for a quality beach-break that's often offshore, at the end of the line south. Across on North Uist, **Hosta** is worth a look, and **Culla Bay** on Benbecula has quality beach-breaks on larger swells and south winds. More consistent but more of a mission is **Vatersay**, on Barra.

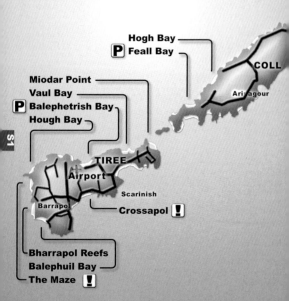

Hogh Bay

P **Feall Bay**

COLL

Arinagour

Miodar Point

Vaul Bay

P **Balephetrish Bay**

Hough Bay

TIREE

Airport

Scarinish

Barrapol

Crossapol !

Bharrapol Reefs

Balephuil Bay

The Maze !

S1

TIREE AND COLL

Your journey starts at Oban, about 95 miles north of Edinburgh. The ferry takes about 3 hours to Arinagour on Coll and another hour to Tiree, where you'll be dropped off at Scarinish on the south coast. Its about 98 quid for a car so take your mates! Accommodation is mostly in rental cottages, and you can get info from www.scotland-info.co.uk.

Tiree is known as one of the windiest places in the UK and claims to be the sunniest. It benefits from exposure to the brunt of the Atlantic's power, and a contorted coastline offering every possible angle to those harsh winds. It is unlikely that you will not find a wave here with at least partially off-shore conditions to match.

Crossapol: Right outside Scarinish and the ferry is a good beginners spot, pretty much flat most of the time but often off-shore and surfable when other spots are maxed out. Shipwreck.

Balephuil Bay: South again from Bharrapol, is a sandy beach protected from north winds, with some quality banks on any south to west swells. On those huge northwest swells it can be one of the only places that lines up on the island. Quality reef/point options at the west end.

Bharrapol: Just past Middleton at the SW end of the B8065 hosts some offshore reefs for experienced surfers on any east wind. A few km north you will find **The Maze**, just near the chapel at Kilkenneth. This place can be flat or huge, but worth a look on northeast winds. It gets big, both beach-break peaks, and the point at the top which is a classic. Both are advanced, and can get big.

Balephetrish Bay: North on the B8068 from Scarinish. Reform beach-break on the inside and an outer bommie way out the back, which holds some size. Likes S-SE winds ideally, on any tide. Rocks everywhere. Advanced.

Vaul Bay: B8069 N from Scarinish then B8069 E. Worth checking on bigger swells and south winds if you want to find an unsurfed reef out past the daunting rocks. Advanced.

Miodar Point: On the north tip of Tiree, a classic point-break that needs just the right swell to work. Take the B8069 E from Scarinish to the end and its left to the end. Intermediate plus.

Back on **Coll**, **Hogh Bay** and **Feall Bay** are worth a look with Feall being protected from the howling south-westerlies.

SALIGO BAY

Islay: You can get to the Island of Islay by ferry from Kennacraig, on the Kintyre Peninsula. From Port Askaig, take the A846 S and go R at Gruinart.

Quality, often heavy beach-break peaks at both ends of the small dune-backed bay. Prevailing westerly winds are on-shore although this conundrum plagues most of the best spots on Islay. It can get big, when major currents make life hard. Consistent. All levels when small. Generally easy-going crowd. If its huge on on-shore SW wind, check out **Ardnave Bay** and point by heading back to Gruinart and taking the road north.

MACHIR BAY

Islay: South around the headland from Saligo Bay, or you can head here by taking the A846 from Askaig and doing a R at Bridgend. Follow through to Machrie and the cemetery.

Mostly beach-break set-ups here with hollow peaks of consequence in any east wind. It takes any swell from the southwest to the north, with solid north-west swells igniting the right-hander at the right side of the beach. It can get heavy here if there's swell, when its for advanced surfers. 2-8ft.

LOSSIT

Islay: A846 from Port Askaig then A847 to Portnahaven. There's a little track/road north to Lossit Farm and Bay, then a major hike.

This semi protected cove has good beach-break action and is quite consistent. It's slightly out of the way so you'll find a mellow scene and maybe nobody out. Picks up swell from all directions. 1-8ft. All levels.

Another west coast gem / Pete Adams

Islay: Keep heading south from Port Askaig on the A846. Well signed. Alternatively Port Ellen is nearer and you can get thee ferry straight there. In this case it's just a few km north to the golf course.

An expanse of beach-break reliability from the airport down to Kintra. Laggan can take any number of surfers and still deliver a hassle-free, uncrowded session. It can have good shape whatever the tide, and holds a fair bit of size although the paddle can be tough. It likes west to southwest swell unless there's a major ground-swell wrapping in.

Some quality lefts can be found at the south end by Kintra, and the Machrie river helps form some nice banks north of the golf course. The rocks by the airport are also a quality option worth checking.

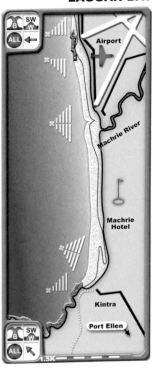

BELLOCHANTUY BAY

Campbeltown on **Mull O Kintyre**. Take A83 north to Westport, then coast road north to Bellochantuy. You'll see it from the road.

North of the village, from the cemetery onwards are a mix of beach, rock and both, with peaks that can hold more swell as you head north. **Graveyards**, opposite the cemetery of course, is mixed sand and

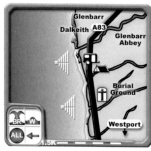

rock for advanced surfers, different peaks for different tides. **Caravans**, by the Caravan Park, is mostly beach break on lower tides, attracting a little less swell than the rest.

WESTPORT

Straight up the A83 from Campbelltown, **Mull O Kintyre**.

The top end of Machrihanish Bay, and working in similar conditions. Lower tides are better for the beach-break peaks, and some of the better banks are found near the rocks. On higher tides, rights can be good with reefs further out if there's enough swell.

More consistent than many breaks in the area. All levels. 2-8ft.

MACHRIHANISH

From Campbelltown on the Mull of Kintyre, head to the village of Machrihanish.

At the bottom end of Machrihanish Bay, this section of beach has a little bit of protection from the south-westerly gales, and there are quality rivermouth peaks especially on lower tides. Strolling up the beach the waves tend to increase in size but you need easterly winds for the open sections.

DUNAVERTY BAY

Located at Southend, south to the end of the B842 from Campbelltown, Mull O Kintyre.

Beach break that only turns it on if the Atlantic swell is very big indeed, or rare Irish Sea energy is running. Southwest winds are straight onshore too, so maths need to be done before making the trip. Low to mid tide is generally best, with high backing off. If you do catch it, there is a rare low tide reef/point setup close to the ruined castle, and you might see it going off. Beginners plus unless the reef is going.

Cold perfection / Lewis Arnold / Pete Adams (below)

NORTH SEA SURF DATA

Background

Scotland's east and north coasts are not well documented yet loaded with quality merchandise in the surf department. While the rest of Europe has been in denial, Scotsmen have been enjoying some of the most awesome waves rideable. The North Sea doesn't benefit from a Gulf Stream injecting warmth and winter surfing is for the truly hard-core only; water varies from 4 deg c to 13 in summer. The north coast and northeast corner are littered with reefs seemingly made by a surfer on high, and they get swell from Atlantic as well as North sea sources. Put simply, these places rock. You will not find better, more powerful waves anywhere in Europe.

When to go

Summer: Unpredictable, infuriating but occasionally perfect, if small. Some primo spots won't even break. **Autumn**: Power swells and often off-shore in the strong southwest winds. **Winter**: Gnarly water temperatures and severe storms. Perfect surf in abundance. **Spring**: A lottery. Coldest water temps.

Hazards

Extreme cold. Storm conditions. Some pollution in built up areas although generally pristine.

M	Swell Range		Wind Pattern		Air		Sea	Crowd
	Feet	Dir'	Am	Pm	Lo	Hi		
J	2-8	wnw	variable	sw	-5	8	4	low
F	2-8	wnw	variable	sw	-5	8	4	low
M	2-8	wnw	variable	sw	1	11	5	low
A	2-8	wnw	variable	sw	4	14	6	low
M	0-5	wnw	variable	sw	6	16	9	low
J	0-5	nw-sw	variable	sw	9	19	11	low
J	0-3	nw-sw	variable	sw	9	19	13	low
A	0-3	nw-sw	variable	sw	9	18	12	low
S	1-8	wnw-w	variable	sw	8	17	11	low
O	2-8	wnw	variable	sw	7	14	10	low
N	2-8	wnw	variable	sw	4	10	8	low
D	2-8	wnw	variable	sw	0	9	6	low

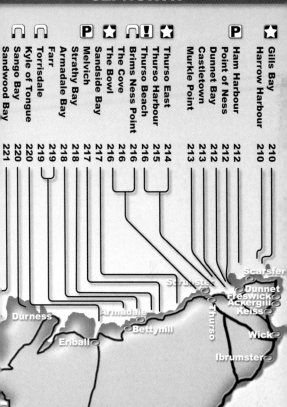

Gills Bay							210
Harrow Harbour							210
Ham Harbour							212
Point of Ness							212
Dunnet Bay							212
Castletown							213
Murkle Point							213
Thurso East							214
Thurso Harbour							215
Thurso Beach							216
Brims Ness Point							216
The Cove							216
The Bowl							216
Sandside Bay							217
Melvich							217
Strathy Bay							218
Armadale Bay							218
Farr							219
Torrisdale							219
Kyle of Tongue							220
Sango Bay							220
Sandwood Bay							221

Scarfser
Dunnet
Fleswick
Ackergill
Keiss
Scrumster
Durness
Armadale
Thurso
Wick
Bettyhill
Eriball
Ibrumster

A9 from Wick all the way to John O'Groats. Turn on the A836 to Gills and turn off R to the pier. Or access from top of headland down path.

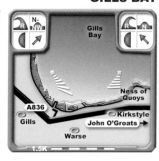

Big NW swell creates super-long, power-packed lefts over rock and stones, which wrap into the bay forming alternating sections; hollow on the ledge, then fat, then hollow again...for up to 600 yards. Awesome. 1/4 to 3/4 tide best. Rs at the Kirkstyle end can also be shapely and hard-hitting. Advanced. Fast ferry to Orkney from here now, for more adventurous surfing at spots like **Marwick**, **Outshore Point**, & **Skail**.

HARROW HARBOUR

Take the same directions as for Gills & go on a couple of miles. Turn R to Loch of Mey. Park in Scarfskerry.

Reef-break heaven, picking up any available swell although nice northwests line up the left-hander perfectly. If a southwest wind accompanies them it can be perfect. Best on higher tides, as rocks pop up at various levels. There's a right/left peak on the other side of the bay. Advanced spot. Can get big.

THURSO Surf

HAM HARBOUR

From Dunnet head north and east on the A836. Half way to Mey, just after the cemetery, is a left up to Ham and a walking track to its "harbour".

Peeling left-hander working best just after low on the push towards 3/4 tide. Sizeable swell needed; it's a rare beauty working outside the now derelict old harbour. It breaks over reef so all the usual caveats apply. It's a little bit of a wander to find this break so check the maths first: Big NW (or very big W) swell, south wind, around mid tide.

POINT OF NESS

Take the A836 E from Thurso to Dunnet. Turn L into Dunnet then L to the pier.

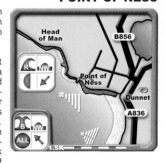

At the top end of **Dunnet Bay** near the pier lies a classic long right-hand point break. Dry hair paddle-outs too. Best 2h after low, up to mid+ tide unless big, when high is also OK. The Point works to 12ft in the right conditions. Advanced. The beach-break peaks which stretch on and on down to Castletown, can be OK on just about any tide. All levels. The whole set-up needs swells from W through straight N.

DUNNET BEACH

Take the A836 E from Thurso to Castletown. Park down at the coastal path & walk to the rivermouth.

The south end of Dunnet Bay is protected from southwest gales, and has beginners beach-break plus a very occasional left tucked in the corner. It takes a decent northwest to west swell to get in, but it is worth a look in these conditions. All levels. An easy alternative to Thurso's more famed breaks, especially when Thurso is blown out. Peaks in middle of beach are better.

MURKLE POINT

From Thurso, head to the tiny village of Murkle, east on the A836. Take a left up to the bay.

Tiny little sandy cove, with a cranking left-hander out the back breaking over slabs of reef. It requires a very big west or northwest swell to do its thing, or a north push, and it offers more protection than anywhere from the southwest gales and westerlies. Mid to high tides good. Can get hairy. Towards Castletown and then left up Battery Rd, you'll see **Nothing Left**, a hard core left-hand reef, and **Indicators**.

THURSO EAST

Take the A9 N from Inverness. At Latherton, turn L on A895. At the jct, turn L on A882 to Thurso. Turn R before the river to Thurso East. Park in the village and scramble over the rocks to the break.

Lined up, often perfect, long reef break that delivers square pits best on very solid west to northwest swells (north more lumpy and fun, but big wests deliver the barrels and often come with nice southerly airflow). On low to mid it's a relatively easy if tight take-off, then an incrementally hollow, fast bowl section. Mid tide is when it hits the ledge at the perfect depth to toss up wide barrels. The reef sits close to your fins; disconcerting on a winters day with the water at 5 degrees and flakes of snow floating about. Summer visitors might get disappointed because the reefs don't pick up swell unless its big, or straight out of the north-northwest. The prevailing south-westerlies are cross-shore so a lot of the time theres a feathered lip firing spray into your eyes. Advanced. 2-8ft plus. Not always crowded, but tight take-off spot means it can't handle numbers. At the turn of the century the middle of the reef was dynamited for boat access, and this area now forms a nasty lump; imagine how long the wave would be if Thurso hadn't been a fishing port! There are quality reefs to be had out in the bay, and around towards Castletown, some of them named and handling considerable size, others hardly ridden.

Thurso East / Lewis Arnold

THURSO HARBOUR: THE "SHIT-PIPE"

Take A9 N from Inverness. At Latherton, turn L on A895 then L on A882 to Thurso. Follow A9 through town to the harbour.

Left and right over flat slab. It's a good spot when the main break at Thurso is crowded out, or too big. It, is easier, and is more protected from the south-westerlies. If Thurso is 6ft, it'll be 3-4ft here. Lefts can barrel if big, and rights usually less critical. The west swells don't get in unless maxing out elsewhere. On it's day, hold downs can nevertheless be severe. The name is a little unfair and there's no effluent although it may look muddy. All levels.

THURSO BEACH

Take A9 N from Inverness. At Latherton, turn L on A895 then L on A882 to Thurso. Cross the river and turn R through town to the car park.

Swell needs to be really big to get in here, but the beach is an easy if lame option if the reef is crowded or too heavy for you. Beginners and kayaks! Not really on the surfing map and for good reason.

BRIMS NESS AND THE BOWL

From Thurso. A836 W & head to Brims Castle. Go past the farm **very** respectfully.

Advanced reef set-up pulling in any swell from W to NE. If it is flat here, everywhere is flat. It's a summer saviour for this reason. Make no mistake, it is not for beginners. **The Point**, on your right, is a lengthy left-hander over a slab of hard flat rock. On NW swells it lines up for long rides and barrels. It's usually the easiest wave here,

is good low to mid tide and fat/no good on high. **The Cove** is a more peaky right-hand reef shouldering out after the initial barrel section. V dredging on low tide but great 2 hours after, up to 3/4 tide. Finally **The Bowl** is a growling hollow right-hand barrel-maker that jacks up fast on a flat ledge close to shore on similar tides to the Cove. The whole set-up handles 2-8ft plus, with 6-8 being perfect. Advanced only. Some major pummelings happen here. Much water moving about and boils so big they have sunk fishing boats.

SANDSIDE BAY

Take the same directions as for Thurso. Follow A836 to Reay. Go R past the cemetery to the car park.

Located next to the Dounreay Nuke plant, this deep bay has some awesome lefts breaking short and fast on middle tides and big swells, liking a very solid west swell best. Rippy beach-break too

over sand, and some rights off the eastern reef. The whole setup is out of the prevailing southwest winds, funneling a westerly round to offshore when Thurso's a mess. It picks up swell from west to northeast. All levels. Nuclear flotsam. Big left indicator bommie out the back, rarely ridden.

MELVICH

Take the same directions as for Thurso. Follow A836 to Melvich. Turn R at the signs for bay & car park.

Awesome, classic lefts into the rivermouth from mid tide up make this a perfect spot on west winds, and a fairly big west to norwest swell. There is a dumping beach / cobblestone break at low tide, a rare (and almost unsurfed) left off the old pier, and a very rare right off the eastern rocks.

Your bases are all covered here and it's off-shore when Thurso is blown out. Brilliant.

STRATHY BAY

The next village W from Melvich. Follow A836 to Strathy. Go through the village. Park near the cemetery.

Out-of-the-way beach-break protected from southwest winds, but receiving more than its fair share of swell. It works through all tides and likes solid northwest pulses. High tide rights pop up off the rocks on occasion, at the east end of the bay but really good lefts reel into the river at 3/4 tide. Uncrowded. 2-6ft. All levels unless big.

ARMADALE BAY

The next village W from Strathy. Turn R off the A836 to the village. Park and walk to the beach.

Nice scenic, secluded, but average beach-break that offers some protection from the wind. Picks up swell from northwest through northeast so a good bet for waves in winter, and rest of the year pretty flat. Rights off the east end of the bay can get OK. Low tide best. Rippy and inconsistent deep bay with swell bouncing off the cliffs and boiling or lumping up.

FARR & TORRISDALE

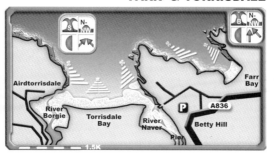

Head W from Armadale on the A836 towards Bettyhill. Turn R just before town to Farr Bay. In Bettyhill there's a car park and you can go to the pier to access Torrisdale. Otherwise, continue on the A836 and turn off R at Borgie to Airdtorrisdale. Various parking spots but please be respectful as surfers have had a mixed history here, with litter and worse happenings of late.

Farr bay is sheltered by a long western head, and is normally smaller than Torrisdale, but cleaner. Nice rights off the right side reef after low tide on the push. Fun fat lefts can form off the west cliffs on mid to high. 1-6ft. All levels.

Torrisdale is a sometimes awesome rivermouth with extensive peaks up and down the beach. Most tides are OK here, with the more protected, less consistent west end often being cleaner and hosting a wicked left-hander. Lined up, long rights are well known outside the Naver by the rocks on the right side of the bay, and A-frame peaks across the strip. This place can really turn on the quality when there's a reasonable northwest swell, southerly winds and a lower tide. Jump off spot on the right side is useful but Scarey on a bigger day. If it is big and messy check Farr. 1-8ft. Swell magnet and saviour when Thurso too small. All levels. Currents if big.

KYLE OF TONGUE

Head W from Armadale on the A836 through Bettyhill to Tongue.

On the east side of the bay at **Coldbackie**, are some reeling rights that need a good rare north swell, and southeast winds. **Talmine**, on the west side will work on a solid north swell and west winds, giving some very very long rides. There can be some good, ridiculously long lefts reeling down the estuary sand on this side of the Kyle. Uncrowded/empty. Very inconsistent and all in all it needs a major swell. Currents. A search. Set your imagination free.

SANGO BAY

Keep going on A838 from Tongue all the way to Durness & the bay.

Beautiful beach-break that is offshore a lot of the time. Sango Bay offers quality sand-banks and peaky rights and lefts, shifting according to tide. A big northwest swell can fire up some nice left-hand barrels on south to west winds, and it's fairly consistent, if smaller than Sandwood a lot of the time. Its the place to go when that spot is big and on-shore.

SANDWOOD BAY

Take the A838 from Tongue to Durness. Take the B801 to Kinlochbervie & Oldshoremore then Blairmore. There's a track N to Sandwood that's only half passable by vehicle; then a long walk.

Long beach with reef and beach-break options at either end, the southern end being the cleanest in prevailing conditions. There are 2 rivermouth peaks as well as whatever the swell is doing there is the chance of a wave here. It is extremely remote so don't go it alone. 2-10ft. Advanced. Currents. Extremely remote and uncrowded of course.

OLDSHOREMORE

Take the A838 from Tongue to Durness. Take the B801 to Kinlochbervie & Oldshoremore. The car park is next to the cemetery.

Fairly inconsistent beach-break that offers quality if the winds are in the north, and a sizeable west to northwest swell is on. Works through the tides, with the beach shrinking considerably at high and sometimes getting more peaky and powerful. All levels. Fickle. Pretty. Quality reef breaks in the area on similar conditions, but not to be surfed alone.

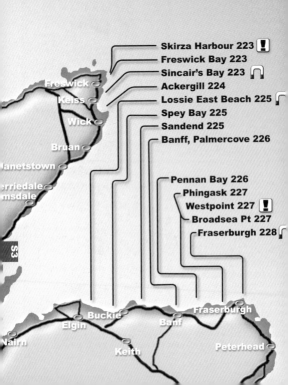

Freswick
Keiss
Wick
Bruan
Janetstown
erriedale
msdale
S3
Nairn
Elgin
Buckie
Keith
Banf
Fraserburgh
Peterhead

SKIRZA

As for Sinclair's Bay. Continue on to Freswick, then R to Skirza. Take the signs R to the pier.

A simply amazing left-hand point wave refracts around and inside Skirza Head, often lining up perfectly all the way to the pier. A big north swell, low tide and northwest to north winds will ignite this spot, although any east swell will get in here. All levels but not easy if big. Dry-hair paddle-out. **Freswick Bay** itself has low tide beach-break peaks holding excellent shape, and some quality rights off the southern rocks from 1/4 tide to 3/4. All levels. Consistent.

SINCLAIR'S BAY

From Inverness take the A9 to Wick. On from Ackergill is the huge Sinclair's Bay.

Enormous beach that regularly delivers quality goods breaking left and right over sand bottom. The north end of the bay - **Keiss**, gets swell from north to southeast, and there's a long boulder strewn left reef-break peak there good from 1/4 to 3/4 tide. Great beach peaks all the way down. The further south you go, usually the more protected it is from south winds. All levels. 2-8ft plus if conditions right. Crowds not a problem.

ACKERGILL

From Inverness take the A9 all the way to Wick. Continue to Ackergill then R past Wick Airport to Ackergillshore.

Heavy reef-break rights featuring heavy take-off as the wave attacks the slab reef, and usually a drop into a substantial bowl section. Needs a good east to southeast swell to wrap so not the most consistent spot around. Advanced.

LOSSIE EAST BEACH

Take A98 W from Banff or A96 E from Inverness to Elgin. Take A941 into town & park near the river.

Good beach-break quality here. Size can increase as you head east so if the river end isn't working there's a heap of beach-break stretching across Spey Bay. It's all off-shore in a southwesterly. Developed area and can get a bit of a pack if good. All levels. Consistent in winter.

S3

SPEY BAY

A98 W from Banff through Cullen towards Elgin. Take A96 then R on B9104. Park in the village/campsite.

Rivermouth and beach peaks that are on all winter. Very shifty and different banks work on different tides, but there is plenty to go around here. Any south wind is good for this spot. Crowds not a problem. All levels. 2-6ft plus.

SANDEND BAY

From Banff, go W on A98 through Portsoy. Turn R on Seaview Rd to Sandend & park at beach/campsite.

Protected cove with some good tame, clean beach-break options. A nice low tide left-hander can work by the harbour, breaking over chunks of reef. Sometimes there's a right on the right side too. All levels. **Cullen**, next door to the west, is another option for more consistent beach-break on any tide and a south wind.

Head W on B9031 from Fraserburgh to Banff. Over Banff Bridge, turn first R to the beach car park.

Rivermouth consistency and plenty of room for manoeuvre on sand bottom. Can get hollow if winds are right, on lower tides. A rare right-hander in the eastern end is quality, relying on a solid north to northeast swell, southeast winds and not too much tide. There's another intriguing right-hander into the rivermouth at **Palmercove Rocks**, definitely worth inspecting while you're there. Trecking west also rewards you with a couple of good reefs.

E on B9031 from Banff or W from Fraserburgh. Park up in the village.

This rock-strewn, pretty little village and cove deals out cobblestone/rock/sand based waves with some good shape. There are 2 main peaks and it can get good here. South winds, north swell, any tide but some better shape on low. 2-6ft. Intermediate plus. Mini boulders to hop over on the way out and in.

S3

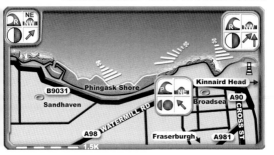

These spots are on the northwest side of Fraserburgh.

Running east from Sandhaven Harbour, **Phingask** is home to some good rocky little breaks, with a left that's well known and often lined up, hollow and fast. This works best on good northwest swells and southerly winds. It's not very predictable, so getting the tide right is a lottery, and often sand movements can move the goalposts. Lower tides generally work better. Rights work here too, and are perhaps better on northeast swells. If you are very nice to the locals, you may be privileged to be shown **Wisemans**, an incredible left-hand winding barrel the other side of Sandhaven Harbour.

At the east end of the above bay, towards Broadsea, you'll see **West Point**, a cranking right-hander running down uneven reef. This awesome spot will not work unless conditions are right however, and higher tides are generally best with some northeast swell. In these conditions it will fire for some distance and get hollow.

Heading back to Broadsea towards the heritage centre, in the small bay with the lighthouse on its eastern tip, **Broadsea Shore** is home to a dangerous, jacking left-hand reef break working on southeast to south winds, solid norwest swell and lower tides. Its one of the more intense spots anywhere, and holds from 3-12ft in the right conditions. Bigger swells break on higher tides. Hard Core only.

227

FRASERBURGH

In Fraserburgh, take Harbour road south past the harbour.

If you are going to get waves anywhere on the east coast, it is here. This lengthy beach faces east to north, and pulls swell from all directions. There is a vast expanse of beach-break all the way down to Parrock Rocks at the bottom of the bay. At this point, known as **Philorth**, south winds are off-shore and there is good shape around the river outlet. Further up towards the harbour are more peaks, and there is a good if fickle left-hander at The Broch, near the caravan park. Breaking over pebbles, this wave lines up perfectly in a north swell on higher tides and west winds to create barrel opportunities and a good chance of a drilling. If it's on there will be a local crew who have waited patiently for this moment so bear that in mind. More surfers here than anywhere, but the crowds are well handled as so many

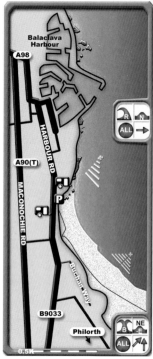

waves in the area. **Inverallochy** and **Charlestown**, to the south, offer up some reef and beach options too, worth the excursion from here, and a little quieter and cleaner.

228

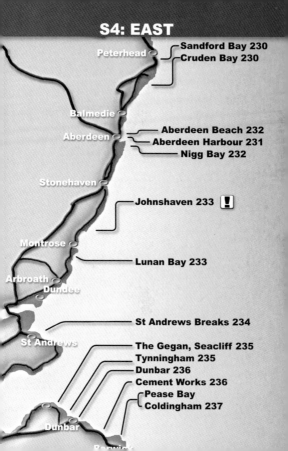

S4: EAST

Peterhead
- Sandford Bay 230
- Cruden Bay 230

Balmedie

Aberdeen
- Aberdeen Beach 232
- Aberdeen Harbour 231
- Nigg Bay 232

Stonehaven

Johnshaven 233 ⚠

Montrose

Lunan Bay 233

Arbroath
Dundee

St Andrews Breaks 234

St Andrews

The Gegan, Seacliff 235
Tynningham 235
Dunbar 236
Cement Works 236
Pease Bay
Coldingham 237

Dunbar

Berwick

SANDFORD BAY

Take A92 N from Aberdeen up the coast. Turn R on A952 to Peterhead. R at the roundabout & sewage works & park up. Look for the spaceship!

Smallish L&R beach break on sand with rocks, best at mid-high in big E or SE swells. Left-hander at the top end can get good. All standards. **Peterhead Town Beach** for good fast L&Rs over shifting sandbars in NE or SE swells. Could be worth a trek N to **Scotstown Head** for 2 point breaks, or on to **Rattray Head** for miles of secluded beach-breaks drawing on all available swell.

CRUDEN BAY

Take the A956/A92 N from Aberdeen up the coast. Take A975 thro' Newburgh to Cruden. Walk over the dunes to the beach.

Just S of the harbour wall, in front of the rivermouth, a peaky L&R breaks over the shifting sandbank deposited out of the river & barrels at high tide. Needs a big swell with E or SE in it. The L close to the wall gets hollow at low tide. Both are protected from N/NE winds. There's a v inconsistent R reef near the rocky outcrop at the S end. Intermediate plus spot. Cool vibe & even cooler water!

ABERDEEN HARBOUR

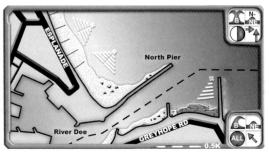

In Aberdeen town centre take the rd S of the harbour round to the south breakwater and park in the car park. For the town beach, head for the Esplanade and park up.

Wedgy rights by the wall in northeast swells, but hazardous situation with boats everywhere and pollution. It needs a lot of swell to work. This end of the beach is protected from southerly winds, and the groynes structure the banks to mould shapely waves on all tides.

All levels, crowds not a problem, currents especially mid tide or when big.

Northern Juice / Pete Adams

ABERDEEN BEACH

In Aberdeen, aim for the town beach. Head for the Esplanade and park up.

A variety of L&R A-frame peaks breaking best in autumn/winter on shifting sandbars. Options include **Fittie** near the harbour wall at low-mid, **Lifeguards** at high tide (due to old ships boiler hazard), **Tunnels** can be a bit bigger and more hollow on big NE or SE swells at mid-high. Beware side shore currents and groynes on high tides. All standards. Search N for similar empty shifting beach-breaks towards **Blackdog, Balmedie** or **Newburgh.**

NIGG BAY

Head S out of Aberdeen round the headland at Girdle's Ness & park at the S end of the bay.

V hollow, fast, barrelling R breaking over man-made boulder reef. Shallow and gnarly at low tide, but works well at mid. Also needs a big NE storm swell to really fire (but the N end will work in a big SE swell). Gets big, and we mean big - well over double overhead, but it needs a strongish SW/W wind to hold the lip up and stop it closing out. All standards.

JOHNSHAVEN

Continue N on A92 from Lunan Bay through Montrose. Head N then follow signs to the village & park at the harbour.

Hard core reef slabs with reeling lefts in a solid northeast swell, and a rare right-hander. You need to be good to surf here; it's hard to access, and worse to get back if something goes wrong.

Try **Inverbervie** for a sheltered bay up north.

LUNAN BAY

From M90 Jct 1, Take A85 then A92 N through Arbroath. Before Montrose, follow the signs to the bay & park at the beach.

A variety of beach break options here, breaking on shifting sandbars. Takes any swell going, and is not too sensitive to tides. Top corner has a left-hander that can really line up, especially on a solid north to northeast swell. Pretty consistent & uncrowded spot, although beware big side shore currents & hefty rips out to sea. Oh, and don't forget your rubber! Intermediate plus.

233

Head N to the M90 from Edinburgh. Take A92 then A915. In town, park off St Mary's St for East Sands & park at N end of town for West Sands.

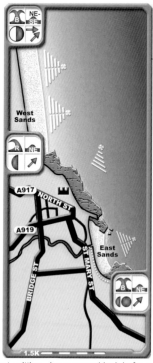

Variety of options here: **East Sands** is home to OK L&R breaks on shifting sandbars. Can get really good in storm swells at 1/4 tide upwards - but the water quality can suffer. All standards.

West Sands is more popular with students, but mellow. L&R's that are long and clean up well in a fresh westerly. All standards. Also gets good, but the banks shift, especially after North Sea storms. Overall a great spot.
Between the 2 beaches - a paddle W round the rocks from the pier at East Sands.

The Reef is a fast, hollow L, breaking on shallow rocky reef bottom. Hard to know whether to call it a surf spot because it usually slams into the rocks. Needs a big NE swell to start spitting - hang on and lock in for a serious barrel if you are a bit mad! The cliffs are an obvious hazard. Advanced surfers only.

THE GEGAN

Head out of Edinburgh E on A1. Turn off onto the A198 coast rd. Head through North Berwick to Tantallon Castle. Park at the N end of the bay at Seacliff.

Mystical setting below the ancient Tantallon Castle at the rocks known as The Gegan. Average L&R beach break on sandy bottom with some rocks, needing a big N/NE swell to wrap into this sheltered bay. Near Edinburgh, but its fickle nature and access time still make it uncrowded. Stunning setting.

TYNNINGHAM

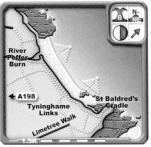

Just past East Linton on A1, turn L on A198 then R on Limetree Walk and a 15min hike to the beach.

Good peaky L&R beach breaks at **Ravenheugh Sands** on rock & sand bottom, best at low-mid tide in a big, running NE swell. Watch your fins at low tide! Intermediate spot at low tide. Walk S for 10mins through the links wood to the rocks & the rivermouth at **St Baldred's Cradle** at the N end of **Tyne Sands.** If you happen to catch it right, there's a fickle L at the point on sandy rock bottom.

235

DUNBAR

From Edinburgh take the A1 coast rd to Dunbar. Take the A1087 & park at Belhaven Bay or John Muir Country Park.

L&R beach break options at **Belhaven**, best in autumn/winter (when there are few tourists because it's cold, of course!) that are great for intermediates & improvers. Best chance of peaky A-frames at mid-high when a solid NE swell is running, but watch the rips. Rumours of challenging rocky reefs in the area of the **Golf Course** & **The Vaults** may tempt travelling surfers to go and explore.

THE CEMENT WORKS (WHITE SANDS)

From Edinburgh, A1 coast rd past the cement works, & turn off at Torness power station. Follow the rd to the bay then R.

N/NE facing bay that is quite hidden away gives good L&Rs on sand & rock bottom. Likes a straight, big NE North Sea swell and high tide, although works in a variety of conditions - a bit inconsistent. Watch out for side shore currents and seaward rips. Hollow and fast with good takeoffs at best. Experienced surfers spot - particularly when it's big.

PEASE BAY

From Edinburgh take the A1 coast rd through Dunbar. Go left as the rd crosses the railway. Park & walk to the bay.

Couple of options at this well-known NE facing spot - R on cobblestones & sand at S end of the bay gives barrel-potential at mid-high. Sandbar Ls at the N end are more mellow, but can turn it on in big swells. Catches all the autumn/winter swell the North Sea can throw at it! Crowded with city surfers but a good vibe. Intermediate plus. Just N is **Reed Point** or just S for **Siccar Point & Wheat Stack** for advanced options.

COLDINGHAM BAY

From Edinburgh take the A1 coast rd. Turn L at the signs on B6438, park up at the bay & follow the track.

Great little bay that serves up good, heavy, hollow L&Rs (mainly Ls) breaking on rocky sand bottom. Best in big storm NE or E swells, when the Ls fire up fast and shoulder-high. Liable to close out - avoid low tide. Tight takeoff zone & can get crowded at weekends with city surfers. Stay in the pubs and enjoy the friendly atmosphere over a few post-surf pints for best results! Intermediate plus spot.

Bundoran / Peter Adams

IRELAND

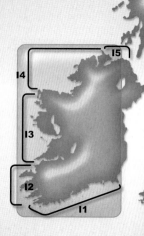

I5

I4

I3

I2

I1

SURF DATA

Background

Some of the most exposed coastline in Europe, bristling with reef and beach-break excellence. Sometimes surfing in Ireland is about finding somewhere small enough to be ridable, and often it's about getting out of the wind, which prevails from the southwest. Well established spots are becoming surprisingly crowded so it pays to explore, and we certainly will not give everything away on the following pages. If the surf doesn't happen there is a rich surf heritage to be imbibed.

When to go

Summer: Can be anywhere from flat to 6ft plus. Prevailing winds are on-shore meaning that exposed consistent spots can be messy. **Autumn**: Predictably, the safest bet for a good surf. Some major swells come through. Often huge at this time although hidden refs and north-facing spots can be going off. **Winter**: A hard core version of autumn. **Spring**: Swell pattern becomes more spread out, and the water is at its coldest, but some great spring sessions are to be had. **Hazards -** Currents. Storm conditions. Isolation. Pubs.

M	Swell Range		Wind Pattern		Air			Sea	Crowd
	Feet	Dir'	Am	Pm	Lo	Hi			
J	2-15	wnw	variable	sw	-2	8		8	low
F	2-15	wnw	variable	sw	-2	8		8	low
M	2-15	wnw	variable	sw	3	11		9	low
A	0-5	wnw	variable	sw	6	14		11	low
M	0-5	wnw	variable	sw	9	16		12	low
J	0-5	nw-sw	variable	sw	12	21		14	low
J	0-4	nw-sw	variable	sw	14	23		15	low
A	0-4	nw-sw	variable	sw	14	23		16	low
S	1-14	wnw-w	variable	sw	12	20		15	low
O	2-15	wnw	variable	sw	7	14		13	low
N	2-15	wnw	variable	sw	2	13		10	low
D	2-15	wnw	variable	sw	0	12		9	low

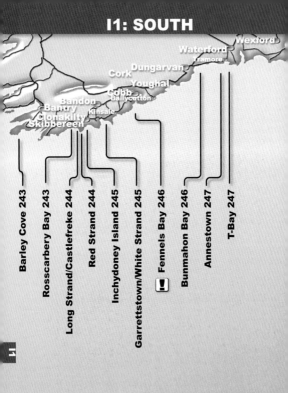

Barley Cove 243

Rosscarbery Bay 243

Long Strand/Castlefreke 244

Red Strand 244

Inchydoney Island 245

Garrettstown/White Strand 245

Fennels Bay 246

Bunmahon Bay 246

Annestown 247

T-Bay 247

BARLEY COVE

Nestled into Mizen Head. From Skibbereen, head through Schull to Crookhaven then due west, past the campsite.

Beautiful sandy bay that is protected from some winds although the pure southwesterly gets onto it quite severely. Beach-break peaks sculpted by rivermouth, and a left-hand reef. Rarely gets bigger than a few feet but a fun place to surf with good shape possible. All levels. Advanced if bigger, and rips by river mouth.

OWNAHINCHY

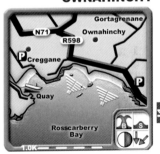

Take N71 from Clonakilty to Rosscarbery. Turn L just before Ross Bridge on R598 to Creggane and Ownahinchy.

Beach-break options on a south to west swell if winds are in the north. Rarely challenging but you'll often find a small wave here in the 1-4ft range. It doesn't hold much more. No loss if you arrive to find it flat, because this is a stunning part of Ireland. All levels. A little bit less busy than nearby spots. Rocks in the middle and to the right.

CASTLEFREKE / LONG STRAND

From Rosscarbery take N71 over Ross Bridge & go R on R598. Go a further 2kms from Creggane to the carparks at Long Strand.

Just round Cloghna Head from Ownahincha going E, reputed to be the best spot in Munster. At best with a good S-SW swell running & a light offshore NE-E wind. Powerful, fast & hollow barreling L&R at the E end, by **Galley Head**, and **Tea Rooms** at west end. Fickle, shifting, on/cross-shore spot drawing the full brunt of the Atlantic so gets rippy & messy. Big crowds & some hassles at weekends. A chill-pill is a must!

RED STRAND

Turn off N71 on R598 between Rosscarbery & Clonakilty. Go through Castlefreke & follow signs for the bay.

This lovely little bay benefits from being in the lee of Galley Head, so it's protected from prevailing SW/W winds (this also means it need a big wrapping SW/S swell to get going). Shifting sandbar peak, most hollow at mid-high. Punchy when on, and watch the cross-shore rip. Crowds appear if the Sou'westers have blown out the breaks to the west.

INCHYDONEY ISLAND

From Clonakilty, follow the signs and head S for a couple of kms to the island and park at the carpark.

Variety of shifting sandbar options including a great left-hander at the eastern end. It can hold the bigger swells when they come in, although rare. Bit more likelihood of one point of the beach being, ideally, light offshore than other south coast spots. Watch for fast-flowing tidal rush at the far West end. All standards of surfer, especially learners/ longboarders.

GARRETTSTOWN / WHITE STRAND

From Kinsale, take the R600 over Kinsale River through Ballinspittle (R604) to the beaches. Carpark at Lispatrick Lower.

Short car trip from Cork makes this place a bustling spot for learners & improvers. The gentle sloping sand (with some rock) bottom generates fickle little peaks on shifting banks. On bigger days there's a reef at the right hand edge of the beach that powers, and can hold 10ft plus. Needs a good SW swell, but storms will blow it out. There's a dodgy little rip on the R hand side too. All standards.

FENNELS BAY

From Cork take N25 then N28. At the roundabout, take the R611 through Carrigaline & R612 to Myrtleville. Go down the steep hill to the sea.

Inconsistent left-hand reef break needing a big south-west ground-swell to line up and bend. Not too easy to find, and not often on so consider it only as part of an extended trip to other spots nearby. All levels. 2-5ft depending on tide. Not hard to surf but rocks about.

BUNMAHON BAY

Take R681 25kms from Waterford or the R675 15kms from Tramore to Bunmahon. Park in town.

One of the more consistent breaks on the south coast, needing N winds (can handle a bit of west in it) and a large S/SW ground-swell. On its day (probably in winter) glassy, fast & powerful L&R sets (mainly Ls) produced by steep-sloping sandbanks. Watch out for rips near the small rivermouth when bigger. All standards, but gets hollow enough for good bodyboard action. Can attract the crowds if it's going off.

ANNESTOWN BAY

R675 10kms from Tramore to Annestown & the beach cove.

Shallow left reef break known locally as 'The Perfect Wave', to the left of the bay. Fast sucky, barrel. Rocks. Worth wearing a lid. Beach-break too. Try heading W to **Kilmurren Cove** for a good, steep, protected break when everywhere else is blown out by winter storms. Beware the strong currents. Advanced surfers only.

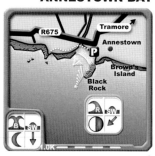

TRAMORE

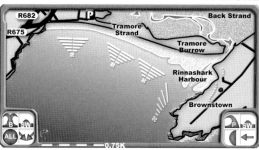

S from Waterford on R675 to Tramore.

Biggest surf club in Ireland, with plenty of heritage. If the banks are working expect nice hollow A-frames that pack a punch. Needs NE winds and good SW swell so often on-shore, but a great spot nevertheless, and healthy surf scene in summer and all year. Lefts at the Brownstown end are magnificent, long and hollow if on.

247

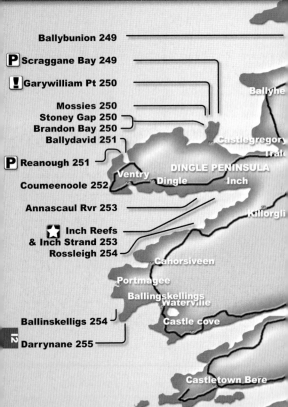

12: SOUTH-WEST

Ballyhe

Castlegregory

Tral

DINGLE PENINSULA

Ventry
Dingle   Inch

Killorgli

Cahorsiveen

Portmagee

Ballingskellings
Waterville
Castle cove

Castletown Bere

BALLYBUNION

Head from Tarbert to Ballylongford, then take R551 for about 15kms to Ballybunion. Park in town.

Mad takeoff spot for this R hand point-like sandbar at the N end of the beach right next to the cliffs (yes, right next!) near the caves (one of the only surf spots on earth where bits of cliff falling on your head is a potential hazard!). Tight takeoff zone but fairly simple to get into - good long walls at high tide. Not always a warm welcome here. Intermediate plus surfers. Other options down the beach. Tight but cool local scene - the home of Kerry surfing.

SCRAGGANE BAY

Take the N86 S out of Tralee for about 15kms. When the road forks, go R on R560 to Castlegregory, then N 6-7kms to the bay.

Welcome to the Dingle Peninsula. As with **Sandy Bay**, just round the corner going E, you'll find small, clean L&R beachbreaks along this long stretch of beach. There'll be a sandbar working in offshore S-SE prevailing winds, all tides and a NE swell. Something for everyone.

GARYWILLIAM POINT & MOSSIES

Take the N86 S out of
Tralee for about 15kms.
When the road forks, go
R on R560 to Castlegreg-
ory, then N 6-7kms to the
point of Brandon Bay. Follow the road to the end
and look for the parked
cars.

Garywilliam Point is
a fast-breaking, hollow
right hand reef break that
starts out in very deep water and jacks up on a shal-
low rocky reef very close to the rocks. A very serious free-fall drop,
followed by a good bottom turn in the pit and tuck in for the spitting-
barrel of your life. Likes a storm NW winter swell, light easterlies
and light-mid tide. Expert psycho-surfers only when it's firing.

Mossies is a mellow but hollow L&R reef break just south of Garywilliam Point, down the cliffs, working in similar conditions. More
a mid-high tide spot. Advanced surfers spot.

Plenty of other great options in this surf-rich neck of the woods:
Dumps is south of these two spots on the way to Sandy Bay. Look
for the gap in the sand dunes.

Stoney Gap is a found further south near the 2 caravan parks.

Brandon Bay itself is home to countless peaks up and down the
long stretch of beach - you'll find something working in virtually
all points of wind/swell.

BALLYDAVID

Take N86 from Tralee to Dingle in the Dingle Peninsula. Take R559 5kms to Murreagh. Follow signs to Ballydavid/Ballynagall & park up.

Good intermediate level R in the north end of **Smerwick Harbour,** near the pier at Ballydavid. Works in big N and NW swells with a straight-forward take off, leading into a long-walled section with a whackable lip. Best at mid tide. Normally uncrowded.

REANOUGH

Continue on the R559 for another 3kms towards Ballyferriter & Smerwick Harbour. R in Ballyferriter to the beach carpark.

The place to head when it is howling with the southwesterly, and swell is big. Needs a pumping straight N swell or some NW in it to wrap in around the Three Sisters headland, which protects the harbour. Hard to get perfect as it needs spot on conditions to work well.

COUMEENOOLE BAY

Take N86 from Tralee to Dingle. Head W on R559 through Ventry for about 8kms till you come to the one of the carparks at the bay.

SW facing beach, open to all S and W swells but favours a big straight S swell & offshore in NE (so can be pretty fickle). Shifting sandbars, big rip currents and deep water make it difficult to read, but at it's best an overhead A-frame of deceptive power in crystal clear water. Most agree incoming low tide is optimum. All standards, intermediate plus when bigger.

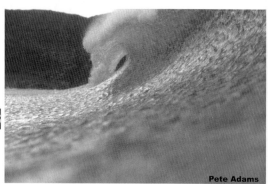

Pete Adams

ANNASCAUL RIVERMOUTH

From Tralee take the N86 Dingle road for 30kms till you reach Annascaul. Take R561 S 1km to the rivermouth.

In dramatic hilly scenery, the rivermouth inlet is home to a well-respected, fast hollow wave, best in big SW swells with a NW or NE wind to hold the face up. Often on or side-shore, but when on it's a good'un with fast take-off and speedy sections. Mid tide incoming is best. Hard paddle-out if big. Advanced.

INCH

From Dingle head E on the scenic N86 through Annascaul to Inch (or from Castlemaine take the R561 heading W.

Park up at the carpark at the N end of **Inch Strand** and the **Reefs** are a slippery climb down the steep track under the cliffs. Takes SW swells, but can work in S or big due W if conditions are right. Light off-shores a must. Fickle but classy R handers with fast takeoff over shallow rock reef, followed by very long (up to 500m), clean walling section. Heavy currents and long paddle. You'll find breaks up & down the strand in straight W swells. Gets smaller as you head S. Good learner spot.

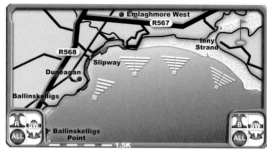

Take N70 from Kenmare all the way to Waterville in County Kerry. Waterville is right in the centre of Ballinskelligs Bay. From there, head N on N70 then L on R567 to Inny Strand, or R566 to Ballinskelligs.

Large bowling bay at the SW tip of the Iveragh Peninsula off the famous Ring of Kerry scenic route. You are in the Gaeltacht, so Irish is the language here.

If there's swell from the southwest to south, this bay will draw it in and produce some fun beach-break action. Rarely hollow, in fact often spilling and fat, it lends itself to improvers. Another benefit is the huge expanse of peaks absorbing any number of surfers. The right side of the bay has some beach/reef options worth exploring towards Emlaghmore west. It can get big, around 8ft if there is swell. Uncrowded.

Dungeagan, on the far west side of the bay, is worth investigating for rare hollow right-handers.

Head N on the Ring of Kerry for **Rossleigh Strand,** for more beach-break options.

DARRYNANE BAY

Take N70 from Kenmare through Sneem as far as Caherdaniel. Go another 2kms then L to the bay & park up.

Needs a straight SW swell running into this stunning, sheltered little bay, not too big as it maxes out at 5ft here. L&R peak near the harbour breaking on gently sloping sandy bottom and a heavier L&R (longer Ls) at the far end with a strong rip to get you out-back. Offshore in a NE wind so it's inconsistent & more than likely a bit mushy. Great little learners spot - intermediate plus at the far end. There's even a surf school here. Oh, Irish hospitality!

Eugene Tollemache / Eire / Pete Adams

13: WEST

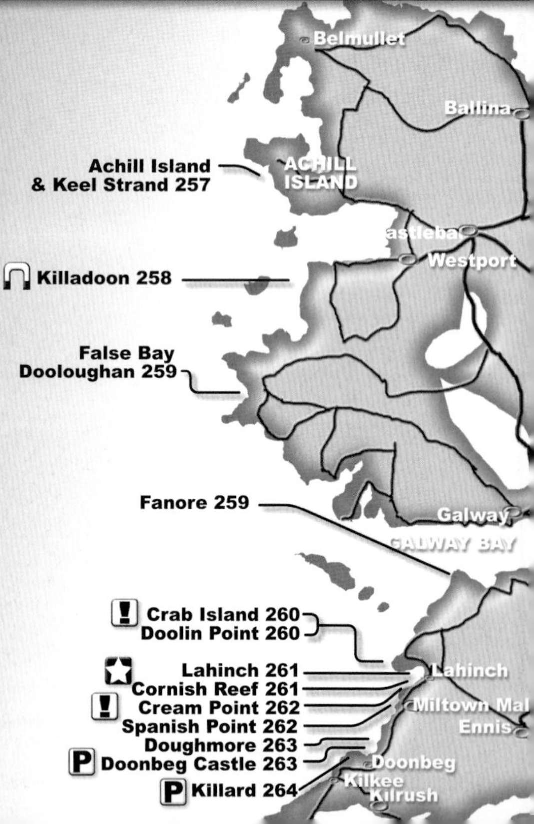

Belmullet
Ballina
ACHILL ISLAND
Achill Island & Keel Strand 257
astleba
Westport
Killadoon 258
False Bay Dooloughan 259
Fanore 259
Galway
GALWAY BAY
Crab Island 260
Doolin Point 260
Lahinch 261
Cornish Reef 261
Cream Point 262
Spanish Point 262
Doughmore 263
Doonbeg Castle 263
Killard 264
Lahinch
Miltown Mal
Ennis
Doonbeg
Kilkee
Kilrush

KEEL STRAND, ACHILL ISLAND

Take the N59 S from Bangor / W from Newport to Mallaranny. Take R319 across Achill Bridge onto the island.

If you're up for real soul surfing, this might just be for you. Once across the bridge, you're in a world of laid-back tranquility, with waves! Sound good? Keel is offshore in N/NE winds. Get it right and it's overhead, although there are currents/rips. Smaller & dropping swells make it very learner/longboard friendly. There's 5 main beaches facing various direction, so options in most conditions - check out **Keem Bay, Dooagh Strand** or **Dooega** area.

Another unknown bit of Eire / Pete Adams

Head S from Louisburgh on R335 for a few kms. Turn R at Tawnymackan & follow the river to Carrownisky or R at Cregganbaun to Killadoon.

Into County Clare now & Killadoon is a great base to explore the many beach-break peaks on the nearby beaches of **Killadoon Beach, Silver Strand, Cross Strand** and **Carrownisky** (where you find Surf Mayo for surf info/board hire etc).

There'll be a wave in all tides & most westerly swells, although be prepared to surf in cross/onshores, as offshore NE/E are rare. 'Relaxed' is an understatement!

2-8ft plus. All levels. Always a way to avoid the crowd (a crowd here is more than 3 people).

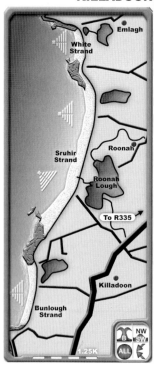

DOOLOUGHAN BAY / FALSE BAY

Take N59 from Oughterard for about 50kms to Clifden. Head S on R341 to Ballyconneely & follow signs.

Surfing in Galway? If you really want to try something different, this is it. These two NW-facing bays are secluded, beautiful spots with golden sandy beaches, adjacent to each other and separated by a hill. Nice little beachbreaks on gentle sandbanks needing big, straight NW swells.

Very friendly locals. There's also rumours of unsurfed reefs just waiting for surf explorers.

FANORE

Take N67 W from Kinvarra to Ballyvaghan. Follow R477 along the coast until you reach the carpark at Fanore.

V much a learner/improver spot, facing due West. Fairly tame & fickle beachbreaks - however, with an offshore E wind & a good NW or W swell, uncrowded 3-4ft clean A-frames can definitely be the order of the day. Not unknown to be sharing waves with dolphins. Only hazards are obvious rock outcrops to keep an eye on at low-mid tide, and the summer crowds.

259

CRAB ISLAND

Follow the same directions as for Doolin to the quay carparks. Paddle out from the pier.

A right like Doolin Point, only bigger, heavier and gnarlier. This is a seriously dangerous board & human-breaking wave, only for the most experienced short & bodyboarders. Best in light E winds & big W swells, (but 3ft and safer in lighter conditions), the wave smashes into a very shallow weedy reef just off the rocks, and can jack up to become a spitting-barrelled beast that can hold 10 genuine feet or more. A long paddleout and back, currents, & peaks can shift. Be warned!

DOOLIN POINT

From Ballyvaghan, take the N67 S to Lisdoonvarna, then the R478 & R479 to Doolin. Follow R459 to the quay carparks.

A quality, hollow R breaks on a shallow, sharp rocky reef at low-mid tide. Has a habit of sectioning or forming different peaks, but with a decent offshore and pumping NW swell, you can expect a fast, hollow, barreling long wave. For the experienced. Many surfers get nailed on the rocks, by sneaker sets and by the fact that it's much bigger out there than it looks (it's also much further than you and your spaghetti arms think!).

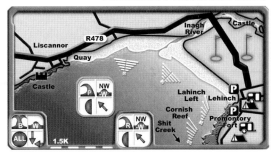

Take the N67 S from Lisdoonvarna for about 12kms to Ennistimon. Continue on the N67 to Lahinch and park in town at one of the two carparks.

You'd be justified in saying that when God made Lahinch, he had definitely just been for a surf! The town itself is home to a great, friendly little surfing community with real heritage. The waves, likewise, providing a challenge for all levels/standards of surfing, starting with **Lahinch Beach** itself: multiple A-frame options on gentle sloping sand bottoms, with a nicely positioned rip on the left hand side. Good for learners & improvers.

Then, as you improve, head left for **Lahinch Left** - a long (and we mean long - 4-500m at best), tubey L which gets pretty powerful in winter and storm swells (a brisk SE offshore wind). You'll get a wave in all tides although be prepared to bail early at low as it's shallow as...expect to share it with plenty of others. Intermediates upwards.

Further left is **Cornish Reef** - another left, working in similar conditions to Lahinch (although more hollow at low). Big, powerful barrels getting double overhead for advanced surfers.

Further left still is **Shit Creek** - in solid swells a hardcore, hollow L at low tide, but great in massive swells at mid-high, for experts. Breaks left and right at mid-high. Experts break. Try heading further south for more macking reef (and a good beach) options.

13

261

CREAM POINT

Continue on from Lahinch on N67 for about 10kms until you get to a sharp L. Take the road R to the carpark at Travaun.

Awesome L&R reef break, breaking close to the rocky shore on a rocky reef. Always bigger than it seems from the shore. If it's on, it's a powerhouse, steep left and right - double overhead and barrelling with quite a pit. It's hollow-faced and thick-lipped at best, at low tide. The hike is across farmers' land so show respect. Ask a local for the form. Experts only.

SPANISH POINT

Take N67 from Lahinch. At the sharp L take R482 into Spanish Point. There's a carpark at the beach.

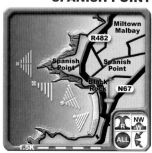

3 point / reefs and an OK beach break in close proximity: **Inside Point** is a consistent short, fast left & right needing bigger W swells to fire; **Middle Point** is a long, steep, barrelling R; and **Outside Point** is a psycho, swell-magnet L&R - only go near it in smaller swells, as it's very hollow, very heavy & the shallow rocky reef is totally unforgiving. Taking one on the head / a hold-down here is guaranteed to ruin your day! Hellmen only. Ongoing access hassles so best behaviour!

DOUGHMORE

Continue on the N67 from Milltown Malbay (Spanish Point) through Quilty and follow signs for the beach.

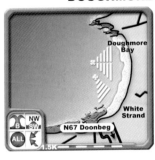

Don't go without talking to the locals - access is a problem with electric fences, angry farmers and all sorts. Very consistent bank going right at the S end, always turns it on even in the smallest swells. When big, it becomes a very dangerous place to surf due to huge water movement (prepare to battle to stay in the take-off zone). Not a place to get in trouble, as the access, rips and the potential hiding you could get in the water, add up to strong surfers' spot only.

DOONBEG CASTLE

About 6-7kms further on N67 from Doughmore. Go through Doonbeg, then R to the slipway near the castle.

What a mystical setting! Needs a monster NW swell to wrap around and hit the reef just near the jetty below the castle. 8-10ft sets can come in and hammer into the very shallow rocky reef to produce a fast, jacking, hollow L. Better in higher tides with a prevailing strong SW. Very rippy when big so good, strong surfers only.

KILLARD

Continue on the road from Doonbeg to Doonbeg Castle for 2kms. Park at Killard near the fort at the beach.

Beautiful, isolated small bay, protected from the unforgiving SW winds and working in similar conditions to Doonbeg. Produces peaky A-frame beachbreaks, best at low-mid tide. Currents run when big. Mellow spot that epitomizes Co Clare surfing for all standards - let's keep it that way.

Solid Eire / Pete Adams

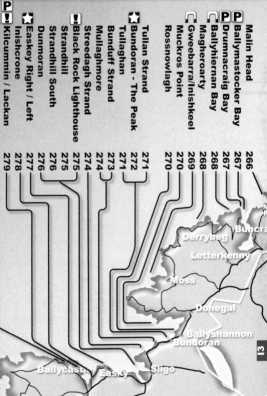

Malin Head — 266
Ballymastocker Bay — 267
Drummacraig Bay — 267
Ballyhiernan Bay — 268
Magheroarty — 268
Gweebarra/Inishkeel — 269
Muckros Point — 270
Rossnowlagh — 270

Tullan Strand — 271
Bundoran - The Peak — 271
Tullaghan — 272
Bunduff Strand — 273
Mullaghmore — 274
Streedagh Strand — 274
Black Rock Lighthouse — 275
Strandhill — 275
Strandhill South — 276
Dunmoran — 276
Easkey Right / Left — 277
Inishcrone — 278
Kilcummin / Lackan — 279
Bunatrahir Bay — 280

Buncra
Derrybeg
Letterkenny
Moss
Donegal
Ballyshannon
Bundoran
Ballycasti
Easky
Sligo
Ballina

13

MALIN HEAD

Head into Co Donegal on either the R238 or R240 to Carndonagh. Go N and then turn L on R240 & go search.

This promontory is exposed to everything the Northern Atlantic can chuck at it. There's a beach/reef option on all points of tides/winds if you check the map.

To start off the long, exposed beach at **White Strand Bay** or the **Back Strand** offer beachbreak options, needing E or SE offshores so consistency can be a problem. Otherwise, **Pollan Bay** at **Doagh Island** may be worth the hike up the beach (park at the beach in Ballyliffin).

All levels. Remote so do not go it alone.

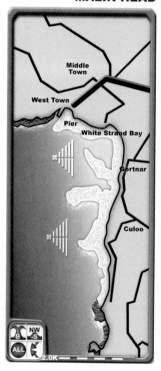

BALLYMASTOCKER BAY

Take R245 N to Millford. Head N on the R246 to Portsalon. Turn R through town & park at the carpark at the N end of beach.

Voted 2nd most beautiful beach in the world. Nice peaky beach breaks get good in large W storms with a straight N swell running. Up to 6 foot peaks in best conditions. Always bigger than it looks though, so keep an eye for sneaker sets. Well protected from the wind & uncrowded. Something for all standards at this magical spot.

DRUMNACRAIG BAY

Follow the R246 N to Portsalon. Go through town and follow the road to Drumnacraig.

More exposed to the swell than Ballymastocker Bay, this small NE facing spot in the lee of Fanad Head dishes up good beachbreaks, similar in size, but is sheltered from the west, so needs more N swell. Pure N, or large wrapping NW swells are best. Consistent in all tides. Again, something for everyone here. Across Loch Swilly, heading W, there's talk of waves for the intrepid around **Dunree Head, Lehan Bay** and **Rockstown.**

BALLYHIERNAN BAY

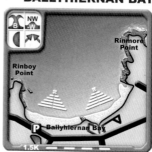

Instead of R to carpark in Portsalon, go straight for 5kms. Turn L on coast road to carpark at the W end.

Most consistent break in this area, open to any W-N swell, the Bay turns on good hollow beachbreaks in most conditions. Only crowded in busy summer season. Even then, no big deal. Weirdly, 2 killer whales spotted here in July 2001! All standards.

MAGHEROARTY

Donegal. Letterkenny Then N56 to Dungloe and Gortahork. Follow coast rd 2 miles N from Gortahork.

Left hand reef break and multiple good quality beach break options. Prefers a pushing tide, and can get pretty hefty when it's big - double overhead a possibility. Generally 3-4 foot. Watch out for the strong currents and rips when it's bigger. Reef break is for advanced surfers, particularly when it's pumping. Very isolated area - surf explorer's paradise. You could bribe a local to take you to a couple of awesome secret spots that have been edited out.

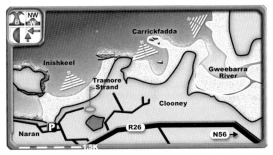

From Donegal, R262 to the N56. L to Ardara, N on R261 10kms to Port-noo.

Spots pick up plenty of swell from SW-NW. Long paddle to a pumping sand-bar at the bay entrance for intermediates. A couple of good A-frame peaks for all standards, a pair of reef breaks too. Beautiful, isolated part of Donegal, home to a variety of great beaches and reef options - try N end at **Traweena** for reef & sandbar options and **Dooey Point** and **Strand**. If you are sniffing out some awesome point-break action, you might be in the right area.

Eire West coast / Pete Adams

14

MUCKROS POINT

Take N56 from Donegal to Killybegs. Take the Kilcar road for approx 10kms, then the Muckros road & park in the village.

There's a small bay at the base of Muckros Head with nice, peaky beach-break options.
However, if you're feeling brave and lucky, go and find the point reef at the Head, breaking on very shallow sharp reef. Well overhead and spitting when big (mission of a paddleout). Strong currents. Experts only.

ROSSNOWLAGH

Between Donegal Town & Ballyshannon, follow signs for Rossnowlagh - you can't miss it.

Many L&R peak options, size up to 6ft. Handles all West swells/tide ranges (arguably best at high) so pretty consistent, this long stretch of beach is ideal for learners & longboarders. Hit Surfers Bar & Smugglers Creek for post-surf yarns & craic. Lessons/hire from the local surf club. Busy in summer. Don't be the subject of the local spectator sport, car-stuck-in-the-sand!

From Donegal, take the N15 for about 20kms SW to Ballyshannon. Follow the N15 for a couple more kms past the military camp. Turn R at KFC, just before Bundoran and park at Fairies Bridge, at the S end of the beach.

Short right peak and a long left from a very consistent sandbar, but other peak options up the beach. Unusual in that it even works in a sou'wester here. If there's no surf at Tullan, chances are there's no surf anywhere on the west coast. The wave refracts off the cliff, doubles up, and forms a wonderful peak with the short right and long, hollow, whackable left. The cliff has claimed a few boards and injured a few surfers over the years - so it's an experienced surfers' spot at the south end. Also, there's a very strong rip adjacent to the cliff so be careful getting in and out - watch the locals if in doubt (never a bad idea to show a bit of respect). If you're a beginner, wander up the beach and surf away from the cliff end. Good chance of a peak to yourself. Great option for those wishing to get away from the more hectic scene of nearby **Bundoran**.

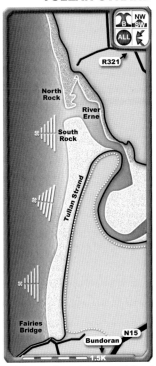

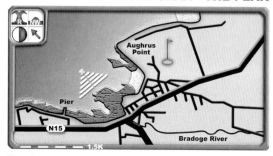

From Donegal, take the N15 for about 20kms SW to Ballyshannon. Follow the N15 for a couple more kms past the military camp into Bundoran. Park in one of the two carparks in town and follow your nose to Waterworld.

One of Ireland and Europe's best waves. A good W swell, fresh S-SE wind and 2 hours either side of low tide, this place is a sight to behold - the legendary **Peak** can be an A-frame left and right reef break of immense power, breaking on rock bottom and spitting both ends! Prepare for a flogging if you get it wrong here - chances are, you will too! One of those spots where sitting out on the shoulder and watch the locals show you how it's done, is cool. Has a habit of breaking boards, people, hearts and, in summer, your constitution, as the water quality can be a bit suss. Rips can be heavy. Do not paddle out here when it's overhead unless you really know what you are doing. Great local scene. Be friendly, show respect and you'll find true Irish hospitality at its best. Think about searching for other options nearby. If it is too intense, or you just want to mellow out, nip round the corner to **Granny's Reef,** etc (ask around).

14

Head W on the N15 out of
Bundoran for a couple of
kms to Tullaghan.

A few years ago this was
considered a bit of a se-
cret spot. However, any-
one staying in Bundoran
for even a short period of
time will know it.
Lovely right hand point,
needing a bit of easterly &
adjacent shorter left hand
point, preferring S-SW to
turn it on. Breaks on boulder rock bottom. Nuff said.
Ensure you follow the letter of the law regarding access over farmers' land - ask around for the form. Advanced surfers spot, respect
for everyone is a must.

BUNDUFF STRAND

Take the N15 W out of
Bundoran for approx
12kms. Turn R at Cliffony
on R279 and park at the
harbour carpark.

Multiple L&R beachbreak
options at this N-NE fac-
ing beach, sheltered from
NW winds. Nicely groomed
lines and 5ft at best. Off-
shore in S-SW winds.
Good spot to surf where
everywhere else is maxed
out when a big westerly
swell is in town. All standards of surfer.

14

MULLAGHMORE WEST STRAND

N15 W out of Bundoran for approx 12kms. R at Cliffony on R279 then first l to the beach.

A number of beachbreak options at the West Strand, working through the tides on any northwest to southwest swell. Way up north there's a whole different proposition at **Mullaghmore Head** - an insane, mysto Left breaking on very shallow rocky reef bottom - Ireland's very own "Mavericks". Genuinely dangerous spot only for experts. Any Size.

STREEDAGH STRAND

Take the N15 W out of Bundoran, through Cliffony & continue for 6kms to Grange. Cross the bridge, turn R to Streedagh and park at the beach.

Pretty good beach break peaks, but suffers from shifting banks and doesn't hold size too well, closing out over 6 foot. Works on any tide. Not normally crowded and open to most swells, so a surprisingly good spot for beginners and improvers. Other options for the intrepid in these parts.

BLACK ROCK LIGHTHOUSE

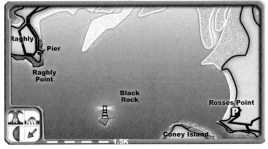

From Sligo, head N on N15 then turn L on R291 & follow signs to Rosses Point. Park up & prepare for a big paddle, or get some sense & get a boat. Hard core experts reef-break in open water.

STRANDHILL

From Sligo, head W on the R292 for 5-6kms to Strandhill. Park at the beach near the surf club.

One of Ireland's best beach breaks. If the banks are just right, you can expect serious quality, very long, hollow and fast, exciting rides. Just watch out at high tide as the backwash is liable to smash the unwary onto the sea defence boulders along the top of the beach. Unsure about conditions, pop into Tom Hicky's (Irish National Surfing Coach) shop on the sea front for local advice.

STRANDHILL SOUTH

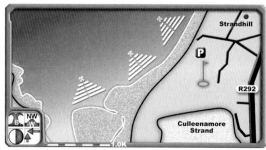

Another part of the expanse of Strandhill. Rivermouth peaks, and a little more protection from the southwesterlies make this section by the golf course worth some exploration.

DUNMORAN STRAND

Head S on N4 from Sligo to Ballysdare and turn off on N59. After about 15kms, cross the bridge. Take next R to the beach carpark.

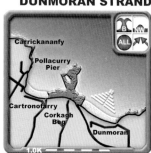

L&R beachbreak options on sand & occasional rock outcrops. Pretty good in a SW gale and best swell is from NW. S SW SE, even OK on a W wind too. Gets up to 6ft in a big W/SW storm. Protected and off-shore when everywhere else is big and onshore.

Uncrowded spot, good for learners and improvers.

EASKEY RIGHT & LEFT

S on N4 from Sligo to Bal-lysdare. N59 for 25 kms to Dromore West. R on R297 for 5kms to Easkey. Just before the river, turn R to carpark near castle.

2 fantastic breaks, justifi-ably known as one of Ire-land's best set-ups - one a Right hand point reef, and, just past the harbour wall, a Left point reef break. Both break on rocky boul-der bottoms at all stages of tide (although low tide makes it even more hollow and heavy). Pure N swell best, but will work with a little NW and W in it too, and needs offshores to avoid slop.

Easkey Right turns on consistently fast, powerful, spitting barrels. The steep takeoff and faces make it a very serious wave, up to 10ft, for advanced/expert surfers.

Easkey Left handles plenty of swell and, again, delivers a steep drop to then barrel and shoulder out nicely. Watch out when it's big-ger for sneaker sets, strong currents and plenty of chat and hassle in the surf. Locals are very protective of their spot, quite rightly, but as with many breaks, the number of surfers in the water here has risen in line with the massive increase in the sport's popularity over the last 15 years. All the usual rules apply. Plenty of other options for the intrepid.

14

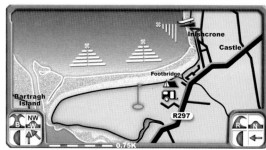

A few km S of Pollacheeny on the R297. Tame beach-break & a long, peeling R over sandy reef. Likes solid N swell, so not the most consistent but good when it's on. Can get busy in summer. Enjoy!

We shall call it...Land Rover Point / Pete Adams

LACKAN BAY AND KILCUMMIN

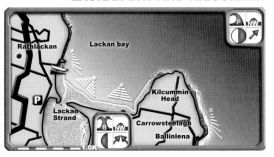

Head N from Ballina on the R314 through Killala. Cross Palmerstown Bridge & take the Rathlackan road. There is a carpark at the bay. For Kilcummin, turn R after Palmersetown bridge. After 3kms, turn R to Kilcummin.

Lackan Bay - Stunning setting - long, golden beach with peaks all the way up, in a beautiful, isolated spot. Pretty consistent - gets going in most smaller N/NW swells. Shoulder-high peaks for all standards are the norm here, best when you get a straight offshore Southerly on all ranges of tide. There's an awesome left-hander in the area. All levels.

Kilcummin - Great, if inconsistent spot (needs spot on conditions to fire). Classy L hand reef break over rock boulder reef at the harbour wall. Head here when there's a SW blowing (it's sheltered from them) & a big winter N swell is closing out everywhere else, for a big, overhead, grinding barrel. Expert surfers break - given the power, rips, inconsistency, spaghetti arms. Hard to get good, but if you do just manage it you won't forget. 3-10ft. Experts.

BUNATRAHIR BAY

Head N from Ballina on the R314 through Killala. Continue for another 10kms to Ballycastle. Either follow sings to the bay, or head through town on R314. Once you cross Killerduff Bridge, turn R to the pier.

Fickle but good quality Left hander breaks on a rocky reef bottom at the far west end of the bay. Best in solid winter N swells. If it is not straight offshore, there's a good chance that it'll be mush.

Golden Celtic sesh / Pete Adams

Tollemache / Eire / Pete Adams

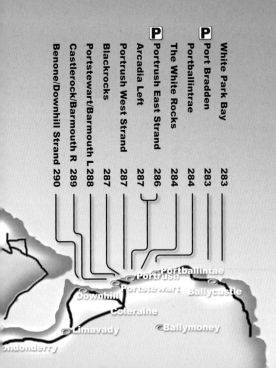

WHITE PARK BAY

Take A2 from Bushmills to Ballycastle. Turn L after 4-5km by the youth hostel & park in the car park.

Beautiful, long beach just past Giants Causeway. More crystal blue water than any other beach in Ireland. Multiple peaks, with good lined up waves at E end. Sand bottom, but some rocky outcrops. Mid tide on the push is best for seriously long winter rides with incredibly powerful banks. Totally consistent. Pretty uncrowded. Most people put off by long walk from the carpark to the beach.

PORT BRADDEN

Take A2 from Bushmills to Ballycastle, 4-5km, turn L by the youth hostel. Park in carpark and walk towards Salmon Fishery.

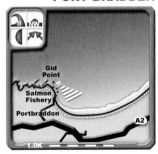

Sheltered L at south end of the beach. Good during westerly gales, when the surf is onshore & maxing out everywhere else. Best at mid tide on the push. Quite shallow, so a good spot to loose a few fins! Intermediate to advanced spot, especially when bigger.

PORTBALLINTRAE

4 miles from Portrush, go L on A2 to Bushmills, Drive past the harbour to carpark at Bushfoot Strand.

N Coast swell magnet - a saviour during summer. When swells are smaller, & everywhere is flat, here it can be 4ft+. Deep water basin & steep shelving beach focuses swell to produce heavy barrelling L&Rs. Some of the best tubes about when it's firing. Renowned for snapping boards & people. Vast crowds on Summer weekends (can be 100 in the water). Better be good if it's over 4ft! The L&R at rivermouth, is v popular with local bodyboarders.

THE WHITE ROCKS

2 miles outside Portrush on the coast road to Bushmills before Tanderagee, turn L just past Royal Portrush Golf course.

Multiple L&R beachbreaks on sandbars (some rocky outcrops at N end). Short, intense & hollow holes - top for barrels/airs. Pretty big swell window, so quite consistent. Can get crowded, but treck up the beach for a perfect peak to yourself. All standards catered for.

On the E side of the Portrush peninsula. Turn into the car park at St Patricks Catholic church on Causeway St. You can't miss the Arcadia.

If this wave is on, it is totally awesome! Very powerful, Hossegor-style beachbreak. Fast, exploding L&R barrels, often spitting. Famed for snapping boards. Consistent good R bank at the end of the promenade. L&R peak in front of the stream. Size 4-6ft is best. Can hold 8ft in winter but impossible to paddle out so advanced surfers run around past the Arcadia, & jump off the rocks. Does get crowded - when the big swells hit the coast, it's protected. Also the least consistent of the N Coast breaks. Watch for strong currents and rips when it's bad - advanced only then.

Arcadia Left is just off the Salmon Fishery. Best at low – mid tide, protected from westerly winds. Good during big westerly storms when all other spots are maxed out. Its cross-offshore here and protected. Can jump off the rocks to save a strong paddle out. Beware experienced surfers only. Get a local to show you how its done, if you can!

Macool's Hostel Portrush 02870824845 www.portrush-hostel.com

PORTRUSH - WEST STRAND

Head for Portstewart, from Metropole corner at lower end of Coleraine Road. First left under the railway bridge, park in the carpark in front of the beach.

A variety of L&R peaky beachbreaks. Consistent, liking a pushing mid tide to really get going. Watch out for sharks (just kidding!) - but note the rocks at the far end of the bay. Being the premier resort on the N Coast, it gets crowded, particularly in summer. Something for everyone here.

PORTRUSH - BLACKROCKS

Located at the western edge of Portrush West Strand.

Classy L hand reef break, reputedly the best on the N Coast, breaks at the western end of the beach on a rocky boulder bottom. Fast, medium-long L, with nice wedgy take-off, barrel section & inside wall for some turns. Best around 4-6ft. Tight take-off zone, & fickle nature (needs exactly the right swell direction to fire). Advanced only.

PORTSTEWART & BARMOUTH LEFT

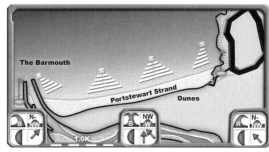

Follow the signs from Portstewart for the strand. At roundabout, pass the golf course on L and head to the beach (owned by the National Trust so summer parking is £4/day unless a member).

Super long beach, almost 3 km, with plenty of peaks up and down - just drive along the beach until you find your own personal play patch. Best spots are on either ends of the strand. Most peaks are consistent when open to N & NW swells. Generally, the walls are not too steep, so it's a good spot for learners/improvers. V popular beach so not uncommon in summer to see 2000 cars on the beach (don't forget to watch the tides & let some air out of your tyres to avoid an embarrassing sinking!)

E end is **Baileys,** adjacent to the town - a sandbar which can produce a super long right. On its day, the longest ride on the N Coast. The take off spot does swing a bit so can be hard to line up. Watch the rips by the rocks. Intermediate plus.

3km down the beach at the W end is the **Barmouth**. A mechanical L peels off the groyne from the River Bann, producing nice walls, not as hollow as other spots but great for manoeuvres. A rip along the groyne acts as a conveyor belt to take you back to the take off zone after your ride, but watch it when it's bigger. Advanced.

CASTLEROCK & BARMOUTH RIGHT

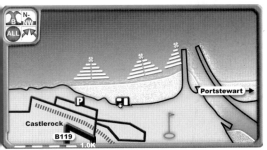

Take A2 W from Coleraine for 5-6 km. Turn L onto the B119 into Castlerock. The beach is well signposted.

Many L&R peaks. Swell magnet. Nice peeling, long waves. Ideal for learners & longboarders. Challenging when big for experienced surfers too. **Barmouth**, at E end of the beach has a R, peeling machine like off the groyne wall for 200m+ when its on. Super-long bashable walls. If tired of going right, paddle across the river & surf the L on Portstewart side. Consistent. Intermediate plus.

Secret Eire / Pete Adams

DOWNHILL STRAND / BENONE

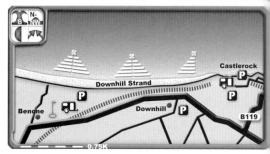

Popular with surfers from Limavady & Derry, follow the coast road for 8 miles from Limavady. Turn left at Benone Holiday complex and follow the signs to the beach.

Tucked in at the E end of Benone, lies a fairly consistent right hand bank in front of the friendly Downhill hostel. This wave can carry for over 150m plus, has steep walls and is sheltered from strong S/SW winds due to its cliffed backdrop. The wave is very uncrowded and over the years many perfect waves have gone unridden here. One of Irelands longest beaches, stretching for over 10km from Magilligan point to downhill. Waves get progressively bigger the further E you go from Magilligan Point. If you don't find an empty peak along this beach then something is wrong. At low tide the beach is very popular with kite surfers, kite buggys and sand yachts etc.

West of the Benone entrance behind the sand dunes lies a British Army shooting range, so check for access restrictions. No car parking fees. Waves here are more rolling & less violent than Portrush or Portballintrae, ideal for beginners and longboarders. From Magilligan Point, surf travellers can take the ferry to Greencastle in Co Donegal, then the R240 to Malin Head for surf.

Eire / Pete Adams

West Country / Pete Adams

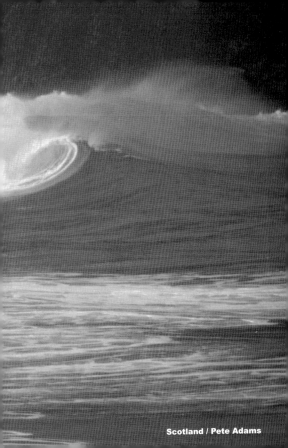

Scotland / Pete Adams

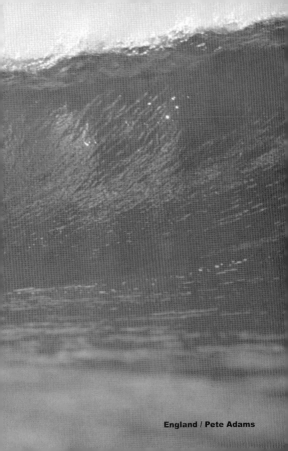

England / Pete Adams

BREAK INDEX

BREAK INDEX

BREAK INDEX

BREAK INDEX

BREAK INDEX

BREAK INDEX

BREAK INDEX

305

SURF FORECASTING SITES

There are so many forecast sites these days...here's our pick of what's available today. For up to date resources, **www.wave-finder.com** has the latest links to all the best sites, for all UK & Eire.

Cornwall
www.a1surf.com/surfcheck-sw-forecast.html
www.surf98.com
www.kneeboardsurfing.co.uk/forecast.htm

North Devon
www.eyeball-surfcheck.co.uk
www.kneeboardsurfing.co.uk/forecast.htm

Northeast England
www.a1surf.com/surfcheck-hartlepool.html
www.magicseaweed.com/forecast.php3

East England
www.eastcoastsurf.co.uk/forecast.html

Channel Coast
www.eyeball-surfcheck.co.uk
www.surf98.com

Channel Islands
www.thebeachjersey.com

Wales
http://fp.pjsurf.f9.co.uk/surfline.html and www.surfsystem.co.uk

Scotland
www.getaforecast.com/surf-scotland.htm
www.northseasurf.com

Ireland
www.surfingireland.net and www.surfsystem.co.uk

Swell model for entire UK
http://facs.scripps.edu/surf/images/euranim.gif

CONVERSIONS AND INFO

Temperature

To convert °C to °F
Multiply by 1.8 and add 32

To convert °F to °C
Subtract 32 and divide by 1.8

Distances

	Multiply by
inches to cm	2.54
cm to inches	0.39
feet to meters	0.30
meters to feet	3.28
yards to meters	0.9
meters to yards	1.1
miles to kilometres	1.6
kilometres to miles	0.6

Finding Wave-finder

Wave-finder UK, USA - Hawaii, Indonesia and Wave-finder Australia are available at all decent surf shops, and surf-friendly bookstores world-wide. For details of your nearest stockist, email info@wave-finder.com or check the site on www. wave-finder.com

We welcome any comments, corrections or questions, and these can be emailed to the same address.

ENGLAND SOUTHWEST

Bath - Just Add Water 01225 425644
Barnstaple
Le Sport Surf Shop 01271 23123
Surfdotcom Internet Cafe 01271 378866 Mail@surfdotcom.co.uk
Braunton
Saltrock Surf Shop 01271 817078 Info@saltrock.force9.co.uk
Chapter Surf Shop 01271 814157
Gulf Stream Surf Shop 01271 815490
Second Skin Surf Shop 01271 812195
Surfed Out Shops - 01271 812512 Info@surfedout.com
Tiki Surf Shop 01271 816070 Shop@tikisurf.co.uk
Bristol
Beachshack 0117 923 2255 Sales@beachshack.co.uk
Sharkbite Surf Shop 01179 299211
Wet & Windy 0117 966 9582 Enquiries@wet-windy.co.uk
The Green Room, 53 Park st, 0117 929 9900
Bude
Surf Spot 01288 352875
Surf Wind N Ski 01288 356156
Zuma Jay 01288 354956
South West Surf Spot 01288 352875
Inthewater Clothing Company 01872 560445 Ck@inthewater.net
Croyde
Croyde Bay Surfing: The Pink Shop 01271 890453
Redwood Surf 01271 890999 Richard@redwoodsurfshop.co.uk
Exeter
Salt City Surf Shop 01392 424015
Urban Surfers 01392 426633
Harbour Sports
Falmouth
Big Wednesday 01326 211159
Hayle - Down The Line 01736 757025
Newquay
Surfers Paradise 01637 877373

Bilbo Surf Shop 01637 878135
Revolver 01637 873962
Boardwalk 01637 878880
Emoceanl Surf 01637 851121 Emoceanl@emoceanl.screaming.net
Fistral Surf Company 01637 850378 Sales@fistralsurf.com
Newquay Surf Centre 01637 873182
North Shore Surf Shop 01637 850620
Ocean Magic Surf Shop 01637 850071
Smile 01637 873389
Sunset Surf Shop 01637 877624
Paignton - Harbour Sports 01803 550180
Penzance - Atlantic Aquasport 01736 65757
South shore surf & skate 01736 365 757
Perranporth
Bathsheba 01872 573748
Piran Surf Shop 01872 573242 John@piransurf.com
Plymouth
Harbour Sports
Just Add Water 01752 600972
City Centre Surfing Life 01752 668774 Surfing.life@virgin.net
Polzeath
Ann's Cottage Surf Shop 01208 863267 - Surfcheck 01208 862162
Tj Leisure Surf Shop 01208 863625
Porthtowan
Sick Lame & Lazy 01209 891881 Info@sicklamelazy.co.uk
Tris Surf Shop 01209 890990
Portreath
savage surf, www.savagesurf.co.uk, 01209 842 920
Beachsavage 01209 842920 Enquiries@savagesurf.co.uk
Reading - Just Add Water 01189 596376
Redland
Crazy Octopus 0117 923 2255 Sales@thecrazyoctopus.co.uk
Saunton - Surfed Out Shops - 01271 812512
Info@surfedout.com
Sennen
Chapel Idne Surf Shop Chapelidne@sennen.freeserve.co.uk
St Ives - Windansea 01736 795560

SURF SUPPLIES

St. Agnes - Aggie Surf Shop 01872 553818
St. Merryn
Constantine Bay Surf Store 01841 520250 Desi@theshop99.fr
eeserve.co.uk
The Pitt, the newsagent, 01841 520 204
Swindon - Just Add Water 01793 496345
Torquay - Two Bare Feet 01803 296060
Totnes - Surfing Classics Fax 01803 866480
Trevone
Rocky Point Surf Shop 01841 5202755
Watergate Bay - Extreme Academy 01637 860 840
Weston Super Mare
Black Salamander 01934 813461 Sales@blacksalamander.com
Woolacombe
Hunter Boardwear 01271 870872 Sales@hunter-boardwear.com
Windsurfers World 0117 9550779
The Bay Surf Shop 01271 870961

ENGLAND EAST & NORTHEAST COASTS

Cayton Bay
Cayton Bay surf shop 01273 585585
Harrogate
Kana Beach 01423 879248
Hull
Wet & Wild Adventure Sports 01482 354076
Kettering
Cygnus 01536 516779
Norwich
Just Add Water 01603 662428
Oshea Surf Design Norwich 01603621166 Paulrob1@lineone.net
Nottingham
Non Stop Surf 01159 531002
Sandsend - Zero Gravity (Whitby) 01947 820660
Saltburn
Saltburn Surf Hire & Shop
H2o Surf Shop 09068 545543 Bwcamfield@aol.com
Scarborough

Fluid Concept 01723 378540 Info@fluidconcept.co.uk
Cayton Bay Surf Shop & Surf School 01723 585585
Secret Spot Surf Shop 01723 500467 Info@seceretspot.co.uk
Skegness - Coogee Surf Shop 01754 898202
Tynemouth
Tynemouth Surf Co. 0191 258 2496 Sales@tynemouthsurfco.sa
gehost.co.uk
Wells-next-the-sea
Orca Mountain Surf & Snow 01328 711722 Orcamountain@btinternet.com
Whitby - Zero Gravity 01947 820660
York
Mayhem, 7 jubbergate, 01904 655 062

ENGLAND SOUTH COAST

Hove - Ocean Sports Board Riders 01273 412241
Boscombe - Sorted 01202 397152
Bournemouth
Sorted 01202 397152 Shaun@sortedboardriders.co.uk
Bournemouth Surfing Centre 01202 433544
Just Add Water 01202 290100
Brighton
Just Add Water 01273 202040
Filf (Rottingdean) 01273 307 465
Surf & Ski Sports 01273 673192
East Wittering - Shore Watersports 01243 672315
Havant - Filarinskis 01705 499599
Poole
Just Add Water 01202 680268
Freeride Surf 01202 675672
Oceanos 01202 701559
Portsmouth - Phish 01705 837062
Rottingdean - Filf Surf Shop - Filf Custom Surfboards 01273
307465 Filfsurfshop@btconnect.com
Shanklin - Offshore Sports 01983 866269
Southampton
Just Add Water 02380 330056
Hythe Marina 01703 843290
Southsea - Radical Styles 01705 873997

Weymouth
Tantrum 07736 014831
Underground surf & skate 01305 789 822 / 761 282
Ocean To Earth 01305 761496

LONDON, EAST AND SOUTHEAST

Covent Garden - O'neill Store 0171 836 7686
Mortlake - Lizzard Surf Company (M) +44 (0)790 992 1880
Canvey Island - Wet'n'dry 01268 510822
Dorking - High Life Surf Shop 01306 881910
Folkestone Activ Folkestone 01303 240110
Guildford - Just Add Water 01483 538293
Kingston Upon Thames Face Plant 0181 296 8989
London
Boardwise 07000 Boardwise
Maidstone - Surf Shack 01797 225746
Southend-on-sea - X-isle Surf Shack 01702 611433
Woking - Surrey Skateboards Ltd 01483-760019

ENGLAND - MIDLANDS

Cannock
The Midlands Surf Centre 0543 505084 Or 0543 570813 -
Manchester
Harpoon Louie's Surf Shop 0161 8399313
Manchester Watersports 0161 839 8988
Tivoli
Walkbig Drop Surf Shop 01792 368861 Shop@big-drop.com
Warwick
720surf And Skate 01926 496046 720@surfandskate.fsnet.co.uk
Sheffield
Lush Longboards 0114 261 9191 Info@lushlongboards.com
Tarleton
Leisure Lakes 01772 814990

CHANNEL ISLANDS

St Peter Port, Guernsey
Sail or surf, 01481 712 621
St Helier, Jersey
Surf Dive'n'ski 01534 36209

WALES

Aberdovey - The Beach House 01654 767030
Abersoch
Abersoch Watersports 01758 712483 Abersoch@watersportstore.com
Abersoch Surf Shop 01758 712365 - Surf Line 01758 712365
West Coast Surf Shop 01758 713067
Abersoch Boardrider.co.uk 01758 713247
Emma@boardrider.co.uk
Aberporth - Wet Spot 01239 811 911
Aberystwyth
Stormriders 01970 626363 Sales@stormridersboardsports.com
Freedom Surf & Sport 01970 612802
Anglesey
Rhosneigr Funsport 01407 810899
Bridgend - Turtle Reef. Bells Rd. 01656 655 526
Broadhaven
Haven Sports 01437 781354
Cardiff - City Surf Castle Arcade 02920 342068
Cardigan - Cardigan Sports 01239 615996
Gower
Pj's Surf Shop 01792 386669 Surfshop@pjsurf.force9.co.uk
Haverfordwest
Game On 01437 779020
Seaweed Surf Shop 01437 760 774
Hot & Glassy 01437 767666 Hotandglassy@.com
Kittle - Gower
Hot Dog Surf Shop 01792 234073
Llandudno - Escape Surfwear 01492 877149
Llanelli - Occy's Surf 'N' Skate 01554 777275

SURF SUPPLIES

Mumbles
Mumbles Surf And Snow 01792-363-169
Newgale Beach
Newgale Surf (Newsurf) 01437 721398
Newport
Adrenalin Surfwear 01633 243825
Pembroke
Waves N Wheels 01646 622066
Porthcawl
Double Overhead 01656 782220
beach break, 00353 5138 6773
Rush Kite & Surf 01656 773311
Simon Tucker Surf Academy 07815 289 761
Porthcawl Marine 01656 784785
Rhosneigr - Fun Sport 01407 810 899
Saundersfoot - Undeground Surf 01834 814484
Southport
Peak Performance Surf & Snow 01704 535151
St Davids
SNS Surf Shop 07866 737935
Ma Simes Surf Hut 01437 720433 Info@masimessurfhut.co.uk
Swansea
Gower Boardriders 01792 459555 Shop@gowerboardriders.com
On Board 01792-547-099
City Surf 01792 654169
Gower Surf Co. 01792 297276
Big drop, 01792 480 481
Tenby
Underground Surf & Skate 01834 844 234
The Edge (01834)842413 & (01554)773720 Info@edgesurf.co.uk

SCOTLAND

Aberdeen
Granite Reef Boardriders 01224 252752 G.forbes@virgin.net
Elgin
Outback Surfing 01343 540750 E-mail Ian@urbanology.demon.
co.uk

Edinburgh
Boardwise 0131 229-5887
Motion 0131 667 2474
Fraserburgh
Point North East - 60 Cross Street 01346 517403
Glasgow - Clan Surf 0141 339 6523
Naturebound, 0141 353 6737

IRELAND

Bangor
Surf Mountain
Belfast
Jackson Sports Tel 028 90 238572 Jackson@sports.totalserve.co.uk
Surf Mountain, 12 brunswick st, 02890 248 877
Bundoran
Surfworld 00353 7241223
Cork
Incide Surf Shop 0214 50 50 77
Tubes Surf Shop (21) 4277 633
Dublin
Great Outdoors 01679 4293
Dingle
Finn Mccool's The Surf Company 00353 (0)669150833
Lahinch - Lahinch Surf Shop 065 7081543
Lisburn
Surf Mountain
Portrush
Troggs Surf Shop 01265 825476 Surf Report 0839 337770
Woodies Surf Shop 01265 823273
Tramore
Beach break, 00353 5138 6773

MY SECRET SPOTS

Name

Directions

Type	Direction	Swell
Tide	Wind	

Description

Name

Directions

Type	Direction	Swell
Tide	Wind	

Description

MY SECRET SPOTS

Name

Directions

Type **Direction** **Swell**
Tide **Wind**

Description

Name

Directions

Type **Direction** **Swell**
Tide **Wind**

Description

WAVE-FINDER
SURF GUIDE - INDONESIA

DATA-MAPS & IN-DEPTH REVIEWS OF EVERY GOOD SURF SPOT IN INDONESIA

WAVE-FINDER
SURF GUIDE - USA - HAWAII

1200 GOOD SPOTS
IN-DEPTH REVIEWS
BREAK DATA-MAPS
SIMPLE DIRECTIONS

**LARRY BLAIR
BUZZY KERBOX**

WAVE-FINDER
SURF GUIDE - AUSTRALIA

WAVE-FINDER 2ND EDITION
100 NEW SPOTS

DATA-MAPS & IN-DEPTH REVIEWS OF EVERY GOOD SURF SPOT IN AUSTRALIA

**LARRY BLAIR
CHEYNE HORAN**

travel.
light on stuff
heavy on knowledge

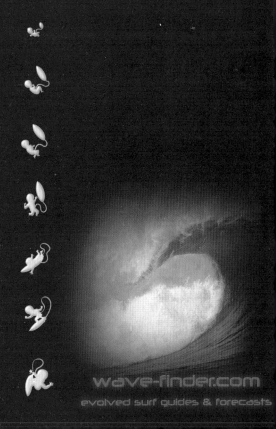

wave-finder.com
evolved surf guides & forecasts